Anupam Kher is an internationally acclaimed actor, director, motivational speaker, and author whose career spans over 500 films and numerous stage productions across multiple languages. A recipient of the Padma Bhushan and Padma Shri—two of India's highest civilian honours—Kher has left an indelible mark on Indian and global cinema through iconic performances in films like *Saaransh*, *Dilwale Dulhania Le Jayenge*, *A Wednesday*, and *The Big Sick*.

Beyond the screen, Kher is a passionate educator and storyteller. He founded Actor Prepares, India's premier acting school, nurturing a new generation of talent. He is also a bestselling author of *The Best Thing about You Is You!*, *Lessons Life Taught Me, Unknowingly: An Autobiography*, and *Different, but No Less: The Unscripted Story behind the Making of Tanvi the Great*, all of which blend personal insight with universal wisdom. Additionally, he has held several prominent positions, including chairman of the National School of Drama, New Delhi, and the Indian Censor Board.

By the same author

The Best Thing about You Is YOU!

Lessons Life Taught Me, Unknowingly: An Autobiography

Different, but No Less: The Unscripted Story behind the Making of Tanvi the Great

YOUR BEST DAY IS TODAY!

ANUPAM KHER

HAY HOUSE

HAY HOUSE INDIA
New Delhi • London • Sydney
Carlsbad, California • New York City

Hay House Publishers (India) Pvt Ltd
Muskaan Complex, Plot No. 3, B-2, Vasant Kunj, New Delhi – 110070, India

Hay House LLC, P.O. Box 5100, Carlsbad, CA 92018-5100, USA
Hay House UK Ltd, 1st Floor, Crawford Corner, 91-93 Baker Street, London W1U 6QQ, UK
Hay House Australia Publishing Pty Ltd, 18/36 Ralph St., Alexandria NSW 2015, Australia

Email: contact@hayhouse.co.in
Website: www.hayhouse.co.in

Cover photograph: Payton Ruddock

First published by Hay House India in hardback, 2021
First paperback edition, 2022
Reprint, 2026
12 11 10 9 8 7 6 5 4 3

ISBN 978-93-91067-40-3 (paperback)
ISBN 978-93-88302-55-5 (ebook)

Printed at Repro India Ltd

FSC
www.fsc.org
MIX
Paper from responsible sources
FSC® C047271

Hay House is committed to a sustainable future for our business, our readers and our planet. This book is made from Forest Stewardship Council® certified paper.

For
My mother, Dulari,
who while dropping me
to primary school repeated every morning,
'Your best day is today.'

Contents

Part V
Moving Forward

Introduction

The urge to write had never been more compelling than the one I felt earlier this year. It came from a place of shared experience and how the difficult times forced us to think and act as one. We collectively fought, and continue to fight, for our survival to emerge as winners from this virus—leaving behind the barriers created by us humans. It left me with an overwhelming emotion of togetherness.

This book had been on my mind ever since I first heard about the novel coronavirus or Covid-19. In my 36-year-long cinema career, I had never taken a day off for the simple reason that when you do what you love and have a deep passion for it, every day seems like a holiday and a day well spent. My friends and family know that I am a restless person and someone who is always on the move—creating opportunities to channel my thoughts and passion. As far as I could remember, even as a school-going child it would upset me when holidays approached. The idea of meeting friends and walking under the clear blue skies on my way to the school liberated me.

I lived in a small, one-room apartment with 14 other family members in Shimla. Although I loved each one of them and enjoyed my time at home, the idea of exploring a different world and experiencing the joys of discovery was exhilarating. Naturally, when the time for self-isolation was upon us, people around me—including myself—could not help but wonder, *how am I going to take up this mammoth task of quarantine?*

However, to my surprise, I learnt and discovered so many more aspects of myself. Gratitude and the value of life took a whole new perspective in my eyes. Listening to the stories of the common man's struggles and the joys of overcoming them on the news drove me to pen down my thoughts.

This book is an attempt to reach out to everyone and share common experiences—a journey of self-discovery, willpower, small triumphs, and the strength of positive thinking. The battle ahead of us is long, but together we will persevere. Our resilience will bring us back on the path of glory. Something tells me that all of us wrote the future during this unprecedented time. A future where the world would be healed . . . a future where the coming generations would look up to us as the pioneers of a healed world.

I arrived in Mumbai from New York on 20 March 2020. While I had been on this journey many a time in the past, that day will be etched in my memory forever.

When I wrote this bit, 30 days had passed since I last stepped out of my house. Four weeks of self-isolation and 720 hours of social distancing. I am going to be honest, there were times when I was upset, bored, and even anxious. But for the most part, those few weeks led me to regain calm and drove me to find the patience needed during the time of chaos and uncertainty.

Looking around, reading the news, and sharing our little stories of success and solidarity compelled me to think about how we, as humans, are the masters of our fate and destiny . . . how we are capable of anything we set our mind to. In the adverse times, we search for the silver lining in the dark clouds and wait for the rainbow after a storm. And while going through it all, we take out the time to appreciate all that this wonderful Mother Earth has generously provided us with.

When the virus started spreading rapidly, we locked ourselves inside the comfort of our homes to not only keep ourselves but also our loved ones safe. We did so to appreciate and give thanks to the thousands of warriors on the front line who were striving to bring back the balance we once drew comfort from. The unsung heroes, right from the cleaners who were out there cleaning our city streets to the bread and vegetable vendors making sure there was food on our tables. From the medical practitioners who continue to fight this pandemic head-on to our police force keeping us safe, leaving their own safety and concerns behind.

I was overwhelmed with the feelings of compassion and gratitude towards all. It had been a journey of thoughts, feelings, and wonder. We had taken life for granted and had assumed that it would always be the same. But it took a pandemic for us to sit back and acknowledge the miracle of life. It took us staying inside our homes to appreciate the smallest act of kindness and made us think of the kind of legacy we would like to leave for the generations to come, too.

I would like to believe that we have gained a deeper look within, a new perspective, and a new-found love and respect for not only the human race but for all the inhabitants of this planet. It has been a reminder of the importance of coexistence and the fact that we share this beautiful planet with many more forces and species. And it is necessary to respect them, value the gifts of nature, and work hand in hand to build a better and safer world—a world where everyone is accepted, loved, and empowered. The year 2020 has provided us with numerous opportunities to turn inwards, find answers, and take up this experience as a challenge. A challenge that might change how we look at life, how we view each other, and how we will treat our home—our planet.

The lockdown not only brought about a change that was much-needed but also laid the foundation of a healed world. And let's not forget the many lessons learnt for the generations to come.

So, while you sit in the comfort of your home and ponder upon current events, life, and many such lessons, I urge you to let those thoughts, ideas, and gestures flow freely. You might not know it now, but we are on our way to make the wrongs right. The world is healing one day at a time, and you, my friend, hold a torch—no matter how small—in leading this world from the darkness into a new light of life.

The famous Welsh poet W. H. Davies once wrote, 'What is this life if, full of care, we have no time to stand and stare.' Now is our time to stand and stare and make this life for everyone fair.

Prologue

30 December 2019

New York City

NEW YORK, ONE OF THE MOST ENIGMATIC cities in the world . . . a city that never sleeps and is always packed with people every hour of the day. As enchanting as this city is, it gets a little lonely as winters approach. Most people leave the city during the holidays to visit their near and dear ones. There is a little less buzz on the streets during this time of the year. One can see mostly tourists roaming around the city, especially at all the prime locations like the Times Squares, the Metropolitan Museum of Art, Central Park, etc. The cold weather creates some kind of gloominess in the air, which can sometimes get to you, especially if you live all by yourself.

My first experience of this city was while I was shooting for the film *The Big Sick* in the winter of 2016. It was then that I felt the energy of this city and the influence it held over millions of people. But it was only when I started living in New York City while shooting for NBC series *New Amsterdam*, in mid-2018, I actually got to experience its magic. New York is truly the greatest cities in the world that leaves you mesmerised. It is said: 'Once you make it to New York, you can make it anywhere in the world.' New York has that kind of effect on you. It changes you completely. It is a city where dreams come true. As the producers of *New Amsterdam* approached me for the role of Dr Vijay Kapoor, one of my incentives for being part of the show was that I would get to live in this city.

Though I was recognised there for the work I had done earlier, I still felt so anonymous, which was great. I have always said: 'Introspection leads you to a path of self-discovery.' And living in New York made me introspect and got me closer to myself. It humbled me and gave me a sense of anonymity, which, in turn, gave me freedom.

Once, during the long Christmas-New Year break from my shoot of *New Amsterdam*, I posted a lot of videos from my Upper West Side apartment of the magical sunrise and sunset that captivate my eyes. And I wanted my Instagram family to enjoy that beautiful view, too. One evening, I was speaking to my manager and CEO of my company, Herman D'Souza, over the phone, and he mentioned how beautiful my sunset video looked. Without missing a heartbeat, I asked him if he would like to come over to New York and spend Christmas in the city. I could sense that he was in conundrum, but I could also feel his excitement.

I told him that I would be happy to host him and his family and they could have a great Christmas vacation. And two days later, he was sitting with me in my apartment, watching the sunset while his son took videos of the magical views outside. Mumbaiites, no matter where they go, carry a warmth within that can sway any kind of coldness away. With his arrival, the coldness of the city was replaced with love and warmth.

That evening, as I was having tea with Herman and his family in my New York City apartment, a news flashed about a certain unknown virus found in China. It didn't grab so much of our attention as we got back to our discussions, giving it very little thought. Next day, the WHO (World Health Organization) reported this issue and there were murmurs around. But people took it lightly since we were oceans away from China.

Dr Li Wenliang, a 34-year-old ophthalmologist at Wuhan Central Hospital, was the first person to identify a rare type of virus called the 'Coronavirus'. On 30 December, Dr Wenliang dropped a bombshell in his medical school alumni group on the popular Chinese messaging app, WeChat. Seven patients from a local seafood market were diagnosed with a SARS-like illness and were quarantined in his hospital. He alarmed the hospital authorities about the existence of a new contagious virus that resembled the deadly Severe Acute Respiratory Syndrome (SARS). Memories of SARS run deep in China, where an epidemic in 2003 killed hundreds of people, which made him take immediate steps of informing the concerned authorities and his relatives. On 31 December 2019, the Chinese authorities informed WHO's China office of the mysterious pneumonia cases in Wuhan.

The word of the disease began to spread in China, but Dr Li's posts were censored. Wuhan Police appeared on Chinese State Television to warn the public about the dangers of spreading rumours. The media urged internet users across the country to not believe online rumours and help build a 'clear and bright' cyberspace. Dr Li Wenliang was detained by Wuhan authorities on 1 January 2020 for 'rumour-mongering'. He was made to sign a statement that he was committing an illegal act by making untrue statements and that he couldn't make any more statements publicly.

Days after he was released, Dr Li returned to work, treating patients who were beginning to flood into Wuhan's hospitals. But on 10 January 2020, he began coughing. Three weeks after he had checked himself into the hospital, he informed his social media followers that he had finally been tested, and that he had contracted the coronavirus.

1 February 2020

As he spent his final days in Wuhan Central's intensive care unit, Dr Li publicly shared how he had warned his friends about the new virus, his ordeal with the police, and his fight with the illness. He revealed that he lived with his wife, who was pregnant at the time, and a young child, and had quickly quarantined himself as soon as he suspected that he was infected. He also informed his followers that his parents were now hospitalised, without disclosing whether they or his wife and child had contracted the coronavirus. But he maintained an upbeat presence on social media and assured everyone that he had his medical license and hoped to leave the hospital as soon as possible. Unfortunately, soon after he was hospitalised, Dr Li succumbed to the coronavirus.

Part I
The Pandemic and Its Perils

1
Grappling with Reality

The year 2020, without a question, has changed the world's perspective in a way no one could have ever imagined! I was in my Upper West Side apartment in New York when I saw the news flashing from different corners of the world, explaining the severity of this new disease that had already claimed hundreds of lives. There was no doubt about the fact that there was an increasing panic amongst the general public. Any new update created more distress and fear among people. Gripped between the fear of stepping out and contracting the novel coronavirus and continuing with normalcy, everything stopped making sense. I didn't realise the intensity of the situation till I became aware of the huge number of deaths in China caused by this novel virus. My thoughts blurred and my eyes looked at my surroundings aimlessly.

The city, which was always bustling with tourists and New Yorkers rushing to work, was eerily silent.

Restaurants that overflowed with people were almost empty, the buzz that the city was constantly enwrapped in was absent, and the only slogan New Yorkers lived by—hustle and never stop—didn't feel the same anymore. My morning walks by the Riverside Park in the Upper West Side became lonelier. I couldn't see my regular laughter club and morning-walk friends.

The daily commute from my apartment to the shooting location of *New Amsterdam* took approximately an hour because of the traffic situation in the city. But as the fear of the virus spread, I started reaching the location within half an hour. The staff at the shoot were constantly checking their phones for any sort of update on this topic. I had been living in New York City for almost two years but everything started to seem strange. It felt like I didn't know the city or, maybe, the city had stopped acknowledging me.

This city felt less and less like 'New York'. The constant updates of the rapid spread of the virus kept people on their toes. The human instinct of survival took over and, suddenly, everything else became a leisure activity—including stepping out of one's house. One morning, I was strolling in Central Park, and it felt bizarre as I had never seen it so empty. I felt deserted . . . unclaimed . . . in a city that I had called home for two years.

Every time I switched on the television, I watched the news filled with fear, after which I calmed myself by saying, 'It's going to be okay.' Several channels displayed a variety of conspiracy theories about the origin of the virus. While most scientists denied any involvement of China in the creation of this deadly virus, the US government kept the media on alert with their in-house findings about the Chinese government developing a biomedical weapon to disrupt the operations of the world's largest economy.

Another conspiracy theory revolved around the involvement of bats as carriers of this virus. For many years around the world, scientists have studied bat coronaviruses by capturing bats in caves and isolating and growing the coronavirus that they carry in tissue culture to observe if they can infect human cells. Called 'gain-of-function research', these studies improve a pathogen's ability to cause diseases so that researchers can characterise its interactions with humans, allowing the evaluation of its potential to cause a pandemic and work on the development of potential therapeutics and vaccines.

Though there is no such proof yet that the virus created had escaped the laboratory, we still base our opinions on what is easiest to believe. Scientists may never be able to track down the origin of the virus or its intermediate host, though it's crucial to track down where the virus came from.

China, on the other hand, has fiercely rebutted all the accusations saying that it's a 'smear' campaign whose primary purpose is to give a boost to President Trump's re-election chances in November 2020. The Chinese government has faced significant criticism, both at home and abroad, over its handling of the pandemic, especially during the early days of the outbreak. However, it has constantly denied any wrongdoing.

The news kept popping up, leading the public in different directions every day, and things kept getting worse. A report by the Department of Homeland Security accused China of concealment and stated that Beijing had obscured the severity of the coronavirus from the world and that it had emerged from a laboratory in Wuhan. Following that assertion, the US doubled its efforts to label Wuhan as the origin of the novel coronavirus, while China opposed the smear campaign with equally harsh response. As a result, US Secretary of State

Mike Pompeo ramped up his attack on China by declaring that there was a significant amount of evidence that Covid-19 emerged from a laboratory in Wuhan.

Along with the accusations between nations and the disruption of local people's life worldwide, the economy slowly began to crash. The fear grew deeper with every new announcement made by the WHO. At that point, the findings and opinions of the WHO were equally confusing. Their constant change in views led to a rage amongst the public.

Slowly, people started wearing masks whenever they ventured outside their homes. Initially, it was a little frightening to watch people in masks . . . as if something devastating was lurking around the corner. People started maintaining a social distance in subways, walkways, and everywhere I went! New York became colder than what it usually was in the winters.

The shoot for *New Amsterdam* was still rolling despite all the buzz the news had created. I was shooting an episode, which coincidentally happened to be on the lines of the ongoing situation in the world at the time. We were shooting for a pandemic sequence, and it was the first time such a word was introduced to my vocabulary.

Soon after the outbreak of the virus in Italy, the entire world was on a precautionary route. Our shoot was cancelled, and the second season concluded with about three episodes short. Processing the ongoing situation and dealing with the gloominess in the world—after coming to terms with the huge number of deaths this virus had caused in China—was difficult and stressful. My heart goes out to all the people who lost their dear ones, leaving a permanent void in their lives.

I have always been punctual with my morning walks in New York. Though I wasn't aware of all my neighbours in the building, we exchanged a friendly smile once in a while when we crossed paths. On day, when I was in the elevator, going back home after a long day at work, the man standing next to me suddenly broke down. I was a bit shaken as I saw him wailing loudly. I couldn't stop myself from asking him the reason behind his emotional breakdown. Initially, he didn't say a word, but as his floor approached, he walked out of the elevator and turned towards me. While trying to hold back his tears, he told me that he had recently lost his best friend in China after contracting the coronavirus. This was my first encounter with the insanity people were dealing with silently.

Along with mourning the loss of so many lives, new developments were hitting me like a hurricane at that moment. Looking at the number of deaths and the helplessness and fear in the eyes of people made me feel uneasy. It is human nature to wait for a silver lining when we are in the midst of chaos and vulnerability . . . we hope to find a ray of sunshine during dark times.

As I wondered how much more the virus was going to affect the world and for how long it was going to stay, my phone rang. A dear friend and fellow New Yorker called me from Sri Lanka. He was visiting his daughter there, and he updated me about the situation of Asia and how much mess South East Asia was already in. He is a jolly human being, but I could sense the stress in his voice, which made me anxious.

My dear friend Anil Kapoor, too, kept me in the loop on the situation in Mumbai. Every phone call he made, he asked me about my plans of coming back home. He wanted me to return to Mumbai as soon as possible. I was a little surprised as I had never seen him so insistent. But that's what friends do—they keep your best interest at heart.

Little did I know that, soon, I would be rushing back home . . .

2
Returning Home

As I have mentioned in the previous chapter, the first time I heard about the pandemic, I was shooting for *New Amsterdam*. It was episode 18 of Season 2 where my character, Dr Vijay Kapoor, gets infected with a virus. He is unwell and needs to be isolated. The other doctors—Dr Max Goodwin (played by Ryan Eggold), Dr Helen Sharpe (played by Freema Agyeman), and Dr Iggy Frome (played by Tyler Labine)—are panic-stricken and chaos is the order of the day. Up until now in the series, my character has always been the caregiver, treating people and saving lives. This particular episode put me in a place where my colleagues have to treat *me*.

A role reversal and all the attention towards my character and the situation at hand got my imagination going haywire. You see, as an actor—and even as a young child—I have always had an active imagination. The reel-life setting got me wondering about a similar real-life situation taking place. I don't take to medical emergencies very well and am terrified of going through an MRI machine as I feel claustrophobic. Thus, for the most part, the uneasiness of what if a reality like this actually transpires settled in my stomach. It was not a very comfortable feeling.

Pandemic. Coming from a Hindi-medium education, my default thinking has been in my mother tongue. I was familiar with the word epidemic, but a new word—and soon a whole new meaning that it was about to present the world with—was introduced to me through my passion, my career, and my work.

We continued to shoot the next day for episode 19 at Kings County Hospital, Brooklyn. I was uncomfortably aware of the murmurs and rumours doing the rounds of an imminent lockdown due to the sudden spread of Covid-19. Our typically enthusiastic and lively unit was overcast with underlying panic and uncertainty. But keeping up with the usual zest, we finished our shoot, and just as we revered in the completion of another episode, it was announced that this would be the end of Season 2. Each season has about 22 episodes, so wrapping up Season 2 at the end of the 19th episode left the team with added confusion and infused more doubts surrounding the situation around the coronavirus.

My assistant, Dattu (Datta Sawant), and I made our way back to the city. A city always bustling with life . . . a city that literally never sleeps . . . wore a deserted look. Closed shops and not many humans in sight made me feel forlorn. It reminded me of Will Smith's movie *I Am legend* and how he and his dog were the lone survivors of a mass destruction. But I shook myself from this feeling and tried hard not to ponder upon this strange emotion and coaxed myself to concentrate on the podcasts I was to record in the coming days. In my head, my plan was simple. 'It's 12th March,' I said to myself. At that moment I decided that I would wrap up my work in New York over the next few weeks and head back home to Mumbai, India, and take it from there.

Plan as we may, a lesson I learnt that day was: Sometimes, the master has better and safer plans for us. As also mentioned in the previous chapter, my dear friend and well-wisher, Anil Kapoor, kept in constant touch with me and insisted that I leave for India as soon as I could. So, on 19 March 2020, I spoke with senior officials in NYC and was informed that there was a possibility of terminating international flights in the near future. The very next thing for me was to get myself home at the earliest.

The Newark airport was surprisingly quiet and subdued. A new accessory—a mask—decked everyone's faces. As I mentioned earlier, due to my wandering imagination and an actor's mind, I tend to view situations and life from a comic point of view—to look at the funny side of things. So, I told myself that it would all be fine soon, that this, too, shall pass. This is how I let my mind treat the word 'pandemic' as a lockdown was not announced yet.

It also brought to my mind the childhood learnings from my father and grandmother. They often said, 'When we dislike a particular person, it gets easier to imagine them with a funny face.' Years later, my theatre director at the National School of Drama, New Delhi, Ebrahim Alkazi, gave us a similar teaching of imagining the audience having donkey faces. It helped tremendously to overcome the fear of performing or stage fright. Practising this technique also helped as a huge stress buster and, maybe, even acted as a defence mechanism of sorts. So, being a pro-life person—not cynical but holding an escapist attitude—my initial thoughts were of a fancy dress or a role-play we all were a part of.

Masks that covered faces and only left the eyes to do the talking left me feeling uneasy, and to be honest, a bit scared as well. Don't we all seek a warm smile or someone's laughter to lift the otherwise sombre atmosphere? Well, out of all the other days, that day, just to look at people without the new compulsion of masks would have been a welcome sight to my panic-stricken soul.

To add to my state of mind, I soon learnt that the first-class lounge was shut and even with a cap and a mask that covered more than half my face, there were people that still recognised me. It was endearing to see them acknowledge me and want to click a picture or two. Soon, I was ushered to another space that allowed me to get my thoughts together and come to terms with the looming chaos.

The journey home had just begun. On boarding the flight, I was met with solemn-looking flight attendants wearing masks, but that did not stop them from greeting each one of us with the same warmth and comfort that one is used to on an Air India flight. Even though I was seated in the first row of the first class, I found myself wondering about the seriousness of the situation. I am usually a nervous flyer, unable to catch more than an hour or two of shut eye on a 14-hour flight. Talking with the flight attendants, the gravity of this pandemic finally began to sink in. They spoke about the news of flights that were being cancelled and the airports that were being closed in the next day or two. I could not help but think about all the stories of people contracting this dreadful virus while flying and at airports . . . about the senior citizens and infants being at a high risk. My mother is 83 years old today (may God give her a long and healthy life), and her presence makes me feel young. I was concerned about her safety and the well-being of my friends and near and dear ones.

My journey from New York to Mumbai was not the one wherein I was in a happy state of mind. Even though I was headed back home after five months, the underlying sense of restlessness, uncertainty of what the future held—not just for me, but for all of us—occupied my mind. I wasn't pondering over '*how will my tomorrow be?*' rather, I was thinking about this unseen, unknown enemy we, as a human race, had to fight.

When it's something we anticipate, like the dangers of falling from a high-rise or a mountain or of an attack from a wild animal, we know the risks as it has a face, and our basic instincts kick in automatically. But how do we fight something that is unknown to us, something we know next to nothing about? What and how do we prepare for something so ambiguous? What precautions do we take? How long do we have to fight it? What extent do we have to go to in order to gain victory against this deadly and mysterious virus? I wasn't paranoid, I was afraid of the unknown. These were the thoughts that decided to occupy my mind during my journey. So, with a small prayer and a lot of positive thoughts, I made the 14-hour flight and landed in Mumbai.

The sight at Newark Liberty International Airport had prepared me little to what sight awaited me at one of the busiest airports in India—Chhatrapati Shivaji Maharaj International Airport, Mumbai. After landing here and taking in the scene, I got extremely worried.

Mumbai airport looked as if it was shut down. Whatever few people were at the airport, hastily made their way towards the exit. Desks, which chimed continuously with the clicking of stamps, were now barren. We are used to the Mumbaikar warmth and charm, and honestly, after the uneasiness I had experienced throughout my flight, I was looking forward to the typical Mumbai-style welcome. However, officials here, too, were going about their day in a pragmatic manner. Each kept to his or her own, and diligently performed their new tasks of screening and checking the temperature of each passenger landing on Mumbai's soil. It was perplexing when I was asked to stand aside after taking my temperature. And when I made it to the immigration counter, imagine my horror when I was called back! I could hear my heartbeat in my ears when I was stamped on my wrist by the authorities that read 'self-quarantine'.

At that moment, I feared I would be hospitalised for 14 days. My thoughts ran amok! There was nothing more I wanted at that time to rush or teleport to the safety of my house, to see the people I loved, and find comfort in their presence. On my way out of the terminal, I was saddened to see the duty-free shops shut. You know it's really serious when shopping is a big no. I made my way out, hoping to see familiar faces that usually awaited my arrival. My manager and CEO of my company, Herman D'Souza, was one of them. But to my dismay, he could not make it to receive me that day. I was happy to see both my drivers, Shiva and Sunil, waiting for me. But the masks on their faces only reconfirmed the seriousness of the situation.

My home is just about 5 kilometres from the airport, but the drive home was disconcerting. It was so because Mumbai's streets were too quiet for comfort—the sounds of cars honking and vendors shouting to sell their wares were absent. They were silenced by an unknown, unseen virus. A virus that would soon unite humankind. It would test our patience, force us on a journey within, and along with it bring about a sea of change. This change was, perhaps, what we needed. How it was presented to us might not be acceptable, but we would learn from it and rise above.

So, on 20 March 2020, I was finally home . . . with the thoughts and feelings that I knew would be the beginning of a new me.

3
Finding My Familiarity in the Unfamiliar

It is not easy to find your bearings when a sudden change takes place. Especially in the midst of such ambiguity where fears swarm and uncertainty lurks. Home is a place that gives one the feeling of familiarity—the usual routine, friendly faces, and the comfort of the walls you are so used to. After the initial jolt of settling in with the word 'pandemic' and wrapping my head around all the rapid changes around me and the world as I knew it, there was nothing more important but to get a feel of homecoming.

When I usually return home, I am cheerfully greeted by my house staff, from my security guard to my domestic help, Madan—who comes rushing down to welcome me. Seeing all the warm and endearing smiles puts me right back at ease and takes away the tiredness of the long flight. But as everything was changing, this, too, was not the same. I could feel the same anxiety, which I had come across during my journey back home, hanging in the air. It was more palpable at home because I was at a place of solace and comfort, which adorned a sullen and worried look. It was as if the normal was taken away, snatched even, due to the gravity of this circumstance.

I am a creature of habit and a stop at my dear friend Anil Kapoor's house just before I enter my home was something I had to let go of. My son, Sikander, and I usually hug when I come back home after months, but this time we just bumped elbows. I spoke with my mother and was asked when I would be visiting her. It was difficult for me to come to terms with the fact that I had to quarantine myself for 14 days, let alone tell my mother the same. It was disheartening to realise that I wouldn't be able to see her and feel her presence around me for some time. It then dawned on me that all of us were going to travel this road together.

However, I couldn't deny my feelings and thoughts of anger, confusion, and frustration. I had a longing to connect with something, anything that gave a sense of normalcy, belonging, and ease in this barrage of silent commotion. In an attempt to calm myself, and as a habit, I entered the temple room.

And there it was! The gods smiled at me, the picture of Maaji was adorned with a garland of flowers, the same lights illuminated the room, and the red cloth were all the same. Finally, a sense of belonging came over . . . I was home, a place where I was the most comfortable.

The only thing that this pandemic had not changed was the smiling face of my gods.

It was the morning of 21st March. But it was not like all the other mornings I have spent at home. Strangely, the usual jet lag felt after a long flight and the change in the time zone was not the same. I wasn't feeling the exhaustion of the journey, rather a funny and surreal sense took over. I woke up to peculiar silence. Living in a city like Mumbai, a city that is always on the move, hustling and bustling with various sounds and nuances, smells and fragrances, one never gets accustomed to the silence. This silence—the white noise—is almost unbearable to a Mumbaikar like me. The only little sounds that claimed the morning light were the slight hush of the leaves in the subtle breeze and the distant chirping of the birds.

I then decided to go for a morning walk. I wanted to calm the storm that was going in my mind that came with the fear of uncertainty. My morning walk seemed out of the ordinary, and I just could not get rid of the feeling that was now becoming louder within . . . the feeling that things were about to change. Again, in search for routine, I called up Anil Kapoor—who stays just one bungalow away—but not knowing when we would be able to catch up face to face and soak in the warmth of casual meetings. I looked at the stamp on the back of my wrist given by the airport officials when I had landed in Mumbai. What surprised me was that this stamp was not like the ones that were more permanent in nature—like the ones that decorated our fingernail after casting our vote in the elections. This could be washed out if tried, but I wanted it to stay a little longer as a reminder to myself that I had to stay inside for not only my safety but for those around me as well. The 14-day self-quarantine needed my attention and this stamp would serve me just that.

While looking at the stamp, I was transported to a memory of a promotion of my film *Hotel Mumbai* directed by Anthony Maras, (the true story of the Taj Hotel terrorist attack in Mumbai) at one of the clubs in New York where everyone received similar stamps at entry. The only difference was that it was fluorescent and glowed in the dark room of the club. Ah! The simple pleasures of being in a crowd, music reverberating as people enjoyed themselves, leaving their worries for another time. I reminisced for a while but as I brought myself back to the present, the numbness continued. I felt the jet lag might finally be catching up and a good afternoon siesta would cure my apprehensions.

Unfortunately, sleep evaded me. So, I got up and unpacked the small temple—the one that I carry with me everywhere, even for a day's journey. No matter where I am, the presence of this temple gives me a sense and security of home and the divine. My assistant, Dattu, usually accompanies me home each time I come back from New York. He has been with me for 35 years now (since 1985), and he helps me unpack and set all my things where they belong. This helps bring back the normalcy of settling at home. But as things were changing then, I felt the uneasiness after he, too, had taken in the restlessness and ambiguity of the circumstances.

His need to be with his family at the earliest, the need to check in with his near and dear ones, and be in the comfort of his world was something I could understand very well. He could not help but request me—for the first time ever—to leave for his home straight from the airport. Amusingly, he even sat in one of the two cars that had come to the airport to receive me and my luggage, hoping I would not convince him otherwise. It made me think a lot more about all of us—the common man struggling to come to terms with the onset of this mayhem. How important it is for us, as regular people, to hang on to any thread of familiarity and safety and the urgent need to keep ourselves and our loved ones safe against an unknown, unseen enemy . . . not knowing what to be prepared for.

I somehow have always felt that what affects the world won't affect India as much. Her resilience and never-give-up attitude have always triumphed all adversities. So, I thought and wished that this pandemic, too, would not affect us as much as the rest of the world, and in a week or two this would be behind us. Not this time my friend! It was on 21st March that Prime Minister Narendra Modi addressed the nation to announce the Junta Curfew. Little did we know that a series of lockdown extensions would continue for weeks.

Modi ji has a very calming and humbling persona. He reminds me of the patriarch who makes the family believe in chasing and achieving their dreams while cheering them on and supporting them in all their endeavours. In his speech, he made a fervent appeal to all Indians to stay indoors as much as possible to avoid getting infected by the coronavirus. He also said that the world has never seen a danger as grave as this. Modi ji also wanted the nation to stand in their balconies and applaud, at 5 p.m. on 22nd March, for the selfless work of the essential services personnel.

Later, the six-week lockdown was announced wherein all the schools, colleges, theatres, hotels, and restaurants would be completely shut. Now, a new word—lockdown—was introduced to me. As an actor, I have always been curious, and I wanted to know the exact meaning of this word. Soon, I found myself excitedly looking for a dictionary. According to the dictionary, a lockdown can be defined as *an emergency protocol implemented by the authorities that prevents people from leaving a given area.* Thus, a full lockdown meant that the people in a given area must stay where they were and not exit or enter another building or area.

That night, I turned off the lights and twisted and turned in my bed with an array of views around this pandemic. Although my mind was flooded with numerous thoughts, for the first time during the onset of this pandemic I felt lonely. I felt anxious and the insecurity of what the coming days would hold was stronger than ever. There was an unsettling feeling in the pit of my stomach. But simultaneously, I realised another important lesson: When something happens that is stressful or hits us like a flash of lightning out of the blue, one whose outcome cannot be controlled and makes our everyday routine and lifestyle come to a standstill, we experience different reactions. Some might take their time to come to terms with it and others might go through varied emotions of anxiety, reactions that could be unpleasant and overwhelming. And a few might dive right into the science of it and collect all the facts possible. Nevertheless, unless we normalise the emotional reactions, we are quite unlikely to engage people in the actions that will help them take care of themselves and adjust to the circumstances.

The Covid-19 pandemic only goes on to stress that it is crucial to explore and build ways that take care of our mental well-being as much as our physical health. And if it is spiritual, skill-building, or even a simple task of spending quality time with our loved ones, stopping to give thanks or a trip down the memory lane can give us the strength to embark on any difficult journey.

It is not always about waiting for the storm to pass. Sometimes, it is about learning to dance in the rain.

4
Thoughts Interrupted

I HAD SET OUT TO WRITE THIS BOOK AS AN account for the lessons we learnt and the positive approach that we took during the time of chaos. An account of everyday life during this time and an uplifting view on life can help one adapt to the times of dismay. This book is a humble effort on my part to make people see difficult times as a learning curve in their lives. Little was I aware that my thoughts and flow would be suddenly interrupted by Covid-19 hitting so close to me and changing my thought process entirely. I had never thought that I would be experiencing it in such close proximity.

On 11 July 2020, a big part of my world came to a crushing halt. My mother; brother, Raju, sister-in-law, and niece tested positive for the coronavirus. My mother was not eating very well, and it concerned us as she would avoid meals stating that she wasn't hungry. My brother and I decided to get her tested on the morning of 11th July to make sure all was well with her. After the tests were conducted, nothing could prepare me and my family for the news that awaited us. We were told that although my mother had a huge cyst in her stomach, which by God's grace was benign, she had tested positive for the dreaded Covid-19.

As the next course of action, my brother Raju and I took the test, too. Imagine my state of mind when his results came out to be positive as well. A part of me felt guilty for testing negative. The sudden need to make sure his family was safe, and that Covid-19 had not spread its fangs to them, we got the rest of the family tested immediately. It was heartbreaking to learn that both my sister- in-law and niece were part of this horror story, too. We were still reeling from the news we had received when the doctor, and maybe rightly so, changed his demeanour instantly. I was asked to stand outside, leaving my family confused and worried. It felt like, all of a sudden, relations didn't count! Comforting a family member and taking time to let the news sink in didn't count! A positive result, somehow, threw out all human emotions.

It was then that my mind drifted to the confusion and helplessness that many were feeling at the same time, perhaps, not too far from where I was standing.

If I, a person of this name and fame could be treated in a matter-of-fact way, I could not help but think about how this virus would be treating others. I was asked to admit my mother to Kokilaben Dhirubhai Ambani Hospital and Medical Research Institute. But I could not gather the courage to tell my mother about her test results as she had been hearing about the dreadful effects of this virus for the last five months. The son in me—and the extreme need to protect my mother at all costs—didn't have the heart to tell her the truth only to scare her. She was told that she only had an infection that needed some immediate medical attention. My mother, being the simple person she is, did not understand the gravity of the situation and kept nudging me to take her back home. In all honesty, all I wanted to do was take her home, prepare her for the journey ahead, and bring her back the next day. But after speaking with Dr Aggarwal, I could see the importance of immediate action.

I fall short of words to explain the heart-wrenching situation I was in.

At Kokilaben Hospital, Dr Singhania was very warm and understanding. During times like these, a simple word of comfort can put an uneasy mind to rest, and I was grateful for his kind words. This young and efficient doctor charmingly acknowledged me and my mother. It was endearing to see him recognise her as the internet celebrity through my videos 'Dulari Rocks'. These are the videos I post of her on social media to give the world a glimpse of this positive, fun-loving, and witty woman that I share my life with. This image of hers and that Dulari does not crumble is what I wanted to maintain.

A million thoughts raced through my head at that time. But somehow, I gathered the strength and began to do things mechanically. It was only when I spoke with the manager and CEO of my company, Herman D'Souza—and he called me back within half an hour, standing outside the hospital to reassure me that all is going to be just fine—that I felt a rush of emotions. Compassion, empathy, and warmth takes on a whole new meaning when those around you reach out when you are going through a difficult time. It is like a beacon of hope, telling you and allowing you to understand that this journey, no matter how tough, will be slightly easier.

Finally, my mother was admitted to the hospital. There was still a look of confusion and doubt on her face and we exchanged a thousand unsaid looks. There was hope in her eyes when she looked at me. It felt like our roles were reversed because, as children, we search for comfort in our parent during difficult times, but here my mother was looking at me and trying to find comfort. Being Anupam Kher, my mother has always taken pride in the fact that her son can make everything easy and understandable for her. I felt like this was one time I was disappointing her as I was searching for answers as well.

I wanted to check with my brother, Raju, and his family. During the brief telephonic conversation, I tried hard to not show my anger as he had gone to a shoot despite the lockdown. My brother was diagnosed with cancer 15 years ago and is a survivor. And even to this day, I can't help but remember the time he broke the news to me. A sudden shock had gripped me, my shoulders went stiff, and I couldn't move. No matter what we go through as siblings, the ups and downs, the good times and the bad, the one thing that only strengthens our bond is the love we have for each other.

While I was ready to leave the room, I could see my mother gain this sudden 'in control', 'I understand' self again. She eagerly asked me to come early tomorrow morning to visit her. It was difficult to see her on the hospital bed, knowing she was fighting this disease.

The next day, the hospital authorities shifted my

mother to the isolation ward without informing me. My mother has been through a lot in her life, be it physical ailments or hardships. But she has always come out a winner. She is my pillar of strength and courage. In my heart of hearts, I knew that she would defeat this, too. After all, mothers are the strongest creatures on this planet—no matter what, they come out stronger than ever.

5
When the Going Gets Tough

It is never easy when your loved ones fall sick. Especially at a time when a virus has terrorised the entire world and everyone is grappling to understand its effect, praying and toiling day and night to win against it. My mother, brother, and his family were tested positive and each one of us picked up our shields to defeat it.

For a mother, her children come first. Although my mother was hospitalised, keeping her own fears and ailment aside, her constant worry was the well-being of her family. To help calm her down and reassure her, we all—including my cousins, my friends Anil Kapoor, and Satish Kaushik—compiled video clippings, requesting her to concentrate on getting better and informing her that all of us were awaiting her return.

The simplicity of Dulari is what makes her this endearing person we all have come to know and love. Mom does not possess smartphones with umpteen applications. She has a simple phone that allows her enough to keep in touch with her dear ones. Hence, Dr Singhania was extremely gracious and made sure that my mother could watch the video. I also feel that the doctor, too, understood the need to put a mother's worry at ease as it could help speed up her recovery.

Those few days were not particularly easy for me, and my mind wandered in different directions. My operating system was full of more fear and doubts, often making me overthink all possible negative situations that could take place. I was informed the next morning by the doctor about my mother's fall as she stood up to place an empty glass on another table. Even though the doctors and staff had well acquainted her with the call bell at her bedside, my mother didn't want to inconvenience them and decided to get out of the bed, which resulted in her fall. I tried to keep calm, not wanting to make her feel awkward, and when she finally spoke to me about her backache, I managed to slip in the information I had received from the doctor. I then requested her to make use of the help not just for her safety but as a gesture of help to all of us. Whenever I called her, my mind played havoc with innumerable thoughts of *will she answer the call or has she fallen, fainted, gotten sicker?*

Every time I called her, I would try and listen to her tone carefully to gauge her recovery status. I remember meeting my psychiatrist, Dr Vishal Sawant, a few years ago in the need to understand my profound sensitivity towards people. Watching senior citizens on the street, or the less privileged, I couldn't help but feel overly sympathetic. It was when he said that my mind made up stories for them, which might not be their truth, but it became so for me. Therefore, I kept telling myself to stop making these stories in my head. I applied the same strategy here. *Anupam, do not make up a story in your head*, is what I would catch myself saying each time I called her and waited for her to answer.

Isn't the brave front we put up at a time like this odd? My family and I put up this brave face and acted as if things were fine. When I spoke with my brother and sister-in-law, Reema, they kept talking about how all was well and how everything was going as fine as it could. My nephew, Pranit, suddenly grew up and was taking up the role of the 'man of the house' as everybody else couldn't do even the simplest of chores. Tables had turned overnight, and the little boy who had been just a kid was suddenly nursing both his parents and sister, Vrinda, back to health.

In the isolation ward, my mother was being the strong woman I had always known her to be as she didn't show even an iota of fear. I, defying the anxiety of it all, pretended to be in control. Testing positive for Covid-19 gave rise to many other distressing concerns, and it could get exhausting and frustrating to keep it together and be strong for one another. It's like a mask of strength that is too heavy to wear. I personally believe that talking about your fears help cope with them as, in so doing, the fear loses its power over you. But keeping up with the mask of strength, in a bid to silence the fear within, how does one then deal with the chaos in the mind? How does one silence the deafening noise of fear tearing into every part of your conscious and subconscious being?

Even with my brother, Raju, being an actor himself, and I being Anupam Kher, blessed with countless support and luxury of knowing the right people, it wasn't easy. I couldn't help but think of the countless faceless people who were struggling, and where the need to step out to put bread on the table and support the family was not something they could afford. They did not have the luxury of taking it slow. A constant battle between your safety and of those you love and keeping the household running and not falling prey to the evils of everyday survival was something not everyone went through. And my heart went out to those who had to suffer due to lack of proper means.

There is another side that comes into play at difficult times like this one. The compassion, empathy, and pure kindness of the people that surround us can do wonders for our mental well-being. I thanked each doctor and staff member at Kokilaben Hospital for their relentless support and more-than-kind ways. Dr Singhania was always in touch with me. His calm and positive attitude had an unexplainable way of keeping my worries at bay. We condition ourselves to think and believe that doctors have everything in control and their personal lives are a far cry from any adversities. But they, just like all of us, are fighting battles of their own. I learnt about Dr Singhania's father having suffered a severe heart attack and going through surgery. But not once did he show it on his face. it was then that I began to understand the mask of strength even more. I asked him about his father's health each day, knowing that a genuine word of care and concern goes a long way.

Anil Ambani's personal involvement in my mother's treatment and his heartfelt statement to Dr Shetty of how my mother was his mother as well, will forever and always be engraved in my heart and mind. Dr Harsh Vardhan, Minister of Health and Family Welfare, on learning of my mother's health, called me each day to enquire about her and my family. He asked me to share Dr Singhania's number with him. Before calling me, he used to take a complete understanding of the treatment and prognosis from Dr Singhania and then took out the time to explain, in detail, the progress and way forward to me.

During such times, when you are fighting to stay positive, to look for some normalcy and a ray of hope, any helping hand adds light to the darkness that surrounds you. A call or even a word of encouragement is uplifting.

The doctors started my mother on a few steroids to help her appetite and aid her recovery. My conversations with her during that time show that the treatment was working as her voice had the upbeat tone to it again—the familiarity of 'Dulari Rocks' that is synonymous with the fighter spirit . . . the optimism and wit that not only inspires this household but the thousands of other grandmothers, mothers, and children who watch her videos. When my family was tested positive and had to self-isolate, I was coordinating with the house chef so that I could make nutritious food available to my brother and his family. It wasn't an easy task, but it made me appreciate the expertise of homemakers.

Finally, after 10 days of extreme pressure and struggle, the doctors informed me that I could take my mother home. Needless to say, this was a challenging time for me and my family, and my perspective to this virus changed completely. But it also taught me the value of staying calm and the magic of compassion and love during adversity.

I knew then that the worst was over for me. But I also realised that it had taught me an invaluable lesson in the miracle of humanity.

6
Dulari Beats the Coronavirus

After all that we, as a family, went through, it was finally time for some good news. I was told by the doctors that it was safe for my mother to be discharged and continue with the home quarantine for the next few days. Relief, happiness, and eagerness took over me, and I couldn't wait to bring my mother back home. Moreover, I was sure that she was aching to come back to the comfort of her house and amongst the people who loved her and cared for her. But at the back of my mind, I was a bit sceptical, too. I wondered whether a few more days of hospital care might help her recover sooner, given that my brother and his family were still recovering back home.

The day before she was to be discharged, in an attempt to understand my mother's preference, I casually slipped in a possibility of her being discharged the next day. I thought she might want to stay a day or two more in the hospital to fully regain her strength. Trust me when I tell you this, I wasn't prepared one bit for the little tantrum Dulari threw even before I had the chance to complete my sentence. She was so adamant on leaving early next morning that she threatened by saying that she would hire a taxi to Raju's house and bang on the door until they opened it and let her in if I wasn't there on time to pick her up. In that moment, the anxiety and fear she must have experienced in all those days dawned on me. I had some idea of the mental toll it must have taken on her as she had no choice but stay away from her family, not have a familiar face around, not have a loved one to talk to, being surrounded by the morbid hospital surroundings, and people checking up on her in personal protection equipment (PPE).

But when I had this conversation with her, I realised the gravity of the mental stress this pandemic flung on all of us. Even today, I get goosebumps when I think about how alone, scared, and lonely my mother must have felt. She put up a courageous front, but I could clearly sense her fear through this little tantrum. That moment, I knew, all the healing and recovering would be much faster once she was home and surrounded by her family.

I spoke with my brother, Raju, that same evening to give him the news of Mother coming back home, and I could instinctively feel his concern. For the most part, he and his wife, Reema, were more than happy to have her back. But as they were facing the same demon, the coronavirus, their concern—and rightly so—was towards their son, Pranit, who was the only member up and about and running a one-man army, catering to all the emotional and household needs of our corona-hit family. We all are extremely sensitive to matters regarding family. It is of utmost importance to be mindful of each other's feelings and thoughts. After all, they are the only ones who stick with you through thick and thin.

Raju and I were brought up with very high values of parents being the supreme power, and for us not hurting our mother—knowingly or unknowingly—has always been of prime importance. It was difficult for me to reassure my brother that our mother would understand the situation and that I would explain to her the need for an extended self-isolation. I could feel his dilemma when he called back, talking about Mom's morning ritual of making her own tea and doing other small things on her own that she took pleasure in. It was a conflict between him and my sister-in-law, knowing how important those little things were for her that were overshadowed by the safety of not only my mother but all the others present in the house. Life can really be tough, especially when you have to decide what *needs* to be done.

Taking all the necessary precautions—which also seem to be the new order of the day—armed in a mask and a cap, I headed to Kokilaben Hospital. I arrived at the hospital before the designated time, as I knew that if I didn't reach the hospital on time, my mother would definitely take a taxi and leave for Raju's house. After having a chat with Dr Singhania, I was all set to take my mother home with me. Before going to her room, I had to complete some formalities. It was reassuring to see how everyone was adjusting to the norms of social distancing while maintaining the same professionalism and warmth. I was sitting quietly but comfortably on a seat with my head buried in phone as I waited for my turn. Just then, a lovely lady, who seemed to be standing in the queue for medicines, turned to me and enquired about my mother's health. I was taken aback by how she recognised me with just my eyes exposed behind all the gear. When I asked her about the same, she was pretty prompt with her reply. She told me that after seeing me in several films, she would recognise me even if my face was fully covered. I smiled at the appreciation. What followed touched me in a way I couldn't ever express. When

I inquired the reason of her being in the hospital that day, I was informed that her husband had a liver ailment. With a warm smile, she turned around and told me that not only was I a good actor but a far better son.

When strangers go out of their way and take the time and effort to compliment someone in a manner so profound, it really strikes a different chord, doesn't it? It makes one believe that there are angels on earth who make other's lives better without even trying to do so. There are people in this world who have no malice in their hearts and only want to spread happiness. Even as we complain about the world turning cold and ruthless, where one has no compassion for the other, its people like this lovely woman, moments like these, and the sheer genuine exchange of warmth and care that restore one's faith in humanity. And even if it was for a minute, I forgot all my anxiety and fear about the future and what this pandemic was going to bring in our lives next.

I approached the cashier with these warm thoughts. He said, 'Don't worry, sir, your mother is going to be just fine. I watch her videos, "Dulari Rocks", and they inspire us all.' It was then that I was hit with another thought . . . another realisation if you may. As actors, performers, and artists, we strike a strong connection with people across the globe. So many people connect with our roles. And maybe that is the reason we are looked up to so much. Dulari, just by being herself, has made thousands of people connect with her. With no formal training or years of experience in acting, just her simplicity and being her true self in those videos, she has garnered immense love and support from my followers on social media. I could not be more grateful for this opportunity of indulging these casual but meaningful conversations with strangers. Yes, these people might be strangers, but somewhere we are connected through the work we do. And it fills my heart with joy that these people love my mother as well.

As I made my way up to the 12th floor of the hospital, where my mother's room was, I decided to record this moment. I asked the nurses at the nurse station to play along and maintain silence. I could see my mother resting while a nurse stood by her side. My mother immediately stirred and turned towards me, full of excitement, as I said my opening line, '*Namaste Maate*'. Her slight movement made the dreary hospital lively for me. Mother could not wait to leave the hospital. And as an old family joke, I asked her, '*Ranga khush?*', to which she replied, 'Ranga khush!'. This is also a little tribute we pay to the great actor Joginder (Shelly) and his 1975 movie *Ranga Khush*.

I couldn't help but notice the nurse's reaction. I could sense that she was reminiscing while watching this banter between a mother and her son. I felt it might have reminded her of someone close, perhaps, her mother and their small secrets that brightened their days together. I learnt that her name was Meenu and she was from Kerala. She was happy to talk with me, and it's always a pleasure to interact with people and give them a small conversation to remember. I asked her if she had watched my Malayalam film *Pranayam*, which means love. She was quick to answer that she had not only watched it but was talking to my mother about it shortly before I had arrived. During the conversation between me and Meenu, my mother was not a least bit interested and wanted to leave as soon as possible. She feared I would change my mind and ask her to extend her stay at the hospital. It was hilarious, but she even refused to sit in the wheelchair, half calculating that if she agreed to sit in it, her son would think of her as someone who was still weak and needed the care provided at the hospital.

On our drive back home, while I was seated in the front and Mom was comfortably sitting at the back, I gently broke the news to her. I finally told her that the reason she was admitted to the hospital was because she had tested positive for Covid-19 and that Raju and his family, too, had tested positive and were still recovering. I informed her about the next few days of self-isolation as calmly and gently as I could. I also explained to her the importance of maintaining self-quarantine rules. All this information, somehow, drained the smile from her face, and she stared out window with a pensive look on her face. This left me feeling extremely uncomfortable.

On reaching my brother's building, I was supposed to drop her downstairs and a house staff was to accompany her to the flat. But my heart melted as I could not bear to let her go this way. So, I accompanied her to my brother's apartment. The big brother in me wanted to desperately see Raju and his family with my own eyes, but I couldn't enter the apartment. I turned to leave and waited for the elevator. At that moment, my mother looked me in the eyes and I could read that she was grateful to God for blessing her with her sons. No, it's not a story that was merely in my head. Every child knows his or her mother, just as each mother knows every heartbeat of her child.

Going through such a difficult time takes a toll on

a person. And it's even more heart-wrenching when your loved ones need you around, but you aren't able to provide the support. As I entered the elevator and the doors closed in front of me, I could finally feel relief wash over me. And for the first time since I had arrived home, I cried tears of respite. My mother was home . . . right where she belonged. Dulari overcame the dreadful coronavirus just as I had presumed. There's no defeating a mother!

Life is not what we think it is and does not always go according to our plans. Life is what we make of it. Each ordeal teaches us valuable lessons. All of us have gone through difficult times during the pandemic, and my personal experience with it compelled me to look back. Only after losing my father, Pandit Pushkarnath Kher, in February 2012, I actually began to see and understand my mother for the person she truly was. Needless to say, she has fought innumerable battles silently.

The lockdown gave me a rare opportunity to sit with her more and hear her intently. During one of our meetings before her hospitalisation, she took me to another room and, very cautiously, explained her wish to gift her jewellery to the family members if something were to happen to her. I was left aghast as the Dulari I knew would not have these thoughts.

In all these years, I have tried my best to give her everything she deserves, the love and time she is entitled to. As a proud son, one day, I thought I would humour her and ask her if there was anything that she needed. To my surprise, she very innocently expressed her wish of owning a house in Shimla—a place where she would spend the rest of her life.

That house is where her heart truly is. Today, that house in Shimla awaits Dulari. And in that house, she would talk about how coronavirus failed in front of a mother . . . my mother!

7
Staying Connected

I think I speak for all of us when I say that living through a pandemic is not something we thought would ever happen in our lifetime. It's been a strange experience and everyone has been affected differently. I tried to get an understanding of this new normal—wearing a mask at all times, carrying a sanitiser everywhere, and not shaking hands or hugging others. It feels unnatural to me. But as they say: 'Desperate times call for desperate measures.'

After the nationwide lockdown was implemented, it was quite noticeable that beneath the silence, the society had been disturbed to its core, and the usual way of life no longer applied. And nobody knew for how long! The fact that this virus had brought the entire world to a complete standstill was growing stronger and stronger in my mind.

In one of the many chats I had with the people around me, I was asked about fear and how I managed to remain optimistic without panicking. Isn't it human nature to feel anxious when things around us are not the way we are used to? Every little change made us realise the horrors of the coronavirus and that it was catching up with us and making us feel scared. A slight sore throat, feeling feverish, or simple lethargy threw, and still throws, us into a downward spiral.

To add to this anxiety, another form of social stigma was attached to being tested positive for the coronavirus. As if the report of testing positive suddenly changed how society viewed us. The news of people, especially the front-line workers, who had tested positive being ostracised by their own neighbours broke my heart. Are we really this cold-blooded? What most of us don't understand is that this calamity has affected many of us physically, financially, and mentally. And all we, as humans, can do is support those who need it the most.

We tend to forget that we live in a community that is largely dependent on one another, and not only for materialistic needs. This is a place where we derive our identity from . . . a place where we welcome our neighbours into our homes. More often than not, it's these very neighbours and friends that come rushing to our aid in time of need. Moments of achievements are celebrated together, and during hard times they become our pillar of emotional support and provide us strength just by being present. Unfortunately, this virus not only managed to set within us the panic of the unknown, but somehow tore us apart from our need to reach out and be there for others as well.

Although the concerns over the rapid spread of the coronavirus are understandable, the labels we gave others—especially during the initial stages of the outbreak—was not. Instead of banishing entire families from entering their residential areas, we should have tried to support them as they were face-to-face with this dreadful virus. While dealing with the pain and fear of the virus, they were also isolated and separated from their loved ones. Imagine their plight when their neighbours refused to even hear them out and treated them as outcasts!

Yes, this fight is meant to be endured alone. But when one is sick and fighting a battle between life and death, the strength is always drawn from compassion, empathy, and support from others. Heaven knows the mind of the person in isolation for weeks—the demons that came out to play, the thoughts that surrounded them, and the fact they were deprived of the most important medicine of all—love and care from the people who matter to them the most.

During a time of immense turmoil, several things usually get outside of our control. In this case, it was about how long the pandemic was going to last and how other people would behave, and what our future was going to look like. It is never easy to accept the unknown, but unfortunately, we have no other way to maintain our sanity. Thinking about how long this situation would last made me anxious and scared. Many of us switched to the internet, with endless hours of searching social media platforms for answers. Some kept watching or reading the news and looked for ways to help bring back some sense of normality. But, for how long? While we cannot decipher a puzzling and scary unknown mystery, we often end up playing infinite scenarios of plausible outcomes, which leaves us drained, restless, and overwhelmed.

It is during such times that we must focus on each other's needs and support our community. Most of our fears and anxiety, which stemmed from this pandemic, came from a place of feeling helpless. Our thoughts and mindset make up a lot for how we perceive what lies ahead. So, give yourself this chance. Make it what you want it to be. Don't let fear dominate your mindspace. After all, we are the masters of ourselves. Hence, the need to do whatever we can, no matter how small, is the biggest need of the hour.

The fight or flight mechanism comes into play, but unless we know, for sure, the right way to work with it—as a community—it could lead to an never-ending feeling of despair and hopelessness. It's important, today more than ever, to keep our thoughts and actions in check.

Humans are social animals. Thus, it's important to stay connected as best we can and reach out for support whenever we need it, even as we cut back on face-to-face socialising. We can have a merry time later with our friends and family because, at the moment, our planet requires something far more important from us. But that doesn't mean we can't be there for the ones who need our love and care.

Coming together as one and standing strong in the face of Covid-19 is something that will take us towards the victory of humanity. Together we will conquer the unseen devil.

8
Fighting Our Inner Demons

After everything that my family went through, I couldn't stop help but think about the deep impact this calamity has brought on each one of us. The coronavirus, undoubtedly, affected all aspects of our lives and the constant news about the pandemic and the rising numbers made us feel restless. Not only did it risk our physical health but also took a toll on our mental health.

Everyone has had different challenges to overcome. Many people were furloughed or fired from their jobs so that companies could keep afloat. Many worked from home, distracted by the news of dangerously rising numbers. Some had to take control of their children's education at home, monitoring their online classes, and most importantly, catering to their emotional well-being while dealing with their own. Unfortunately, not everyone could reach out to their loved ones for support. It has been a trying time for each one of us indeed and all in varied ways.

As we settled into the realities of the pandemic, especially during the phase of unlock, we encountered several feelings, emotions, and thoughts. Many of us tried our best to wrap our heads around these mixed sentiments, which often left us with feelings of despair and anxiety. While understanding the importance of social distancing and self-isolation, we couldn't help but be hit with a wave of emotions, not knowing how to deal with them.

When one is going through a time of adversity, it is important to identify, separate, and acknowledge these emotions and thoughts. I reckon it is completely normal to feel overwhelmed. But I believe the problem arises from the fact that most of us have been trained to ignore the negative emotions and sweep them under the carpet. As humans, we do not like to deal with unsavoury feelings and prefer to move on in life. We find ways to trick our minds and make ourselves think that all is well, and if we do not pay attention to these uncomfortable thoughts, they will magically disappear.

Let me give you an example. When we ask children to not do something, they only get more intrigued to try it out and do it despite our repeated warnings. They keep coming back to it, and over time, it ends up testing our patience and leaves us feeling exhausted. The same applies to our thoughts, too, doesn't it? The more we dismiss them, the more they reoccur and throw us into the tunnel of anxiety and darkness.

On the other hand, when we sit with the child and spend a few moments explaining the dangers of doing something that is not safe for them, we actually help them understand the issue, thereby eliminating the circle of constantly engaging in an exhausting cycle. Similarly, when we acknowledge these feelings and thoughts, only then can we understand their weight on us and articulate them freely. Certainly, sitting with mixed emotions and thoughts can feel as if we on a roller-coaster ride. However, the pandemic presented us with ample time on our hands, making it difficult for us to dodge these thoughts and made us actually deal with them.

One thing that kept coming to my mind was that we all are in this together. While we might be dealing with various responsibilities and duties, one thing that stood out as bright as sunshine was the coming together of the human race. The solidarity, kindness, and compassion we portrayed during the crisis was commendable and heart-warming. My heart was filled with happiness when I saw that while we were struggling and fighting our own battles, we were also making sure to help and support each other in any small way possible. If this is not something to be proud of, I'm not sure what else is.

During the lockdown, I had thought a lot about the experiences we all shared, even if we were miles away from one another. And one of the reasons of writing this book was to share these experiences, making it a medium of support and inspiration in its own way.

Here are a few reminders that I hope would help ease one's struggle during this uncertain time, and, perhaps, in the future as well:

- **Limit the Amount of News You Watch**

  Yes, it is important to stay informed when the world is fighting a battle together. But a constant overdose of news and incessant search over the internet for updates can be overwhelming and add to your anxiety. Instead, schedule some time for news consumption each day. This could also be a time to catch up with your favourite shows and binge-watch them or tick off a movie from your list that you couldn't watch due to your busy schedule. Having a fun movie night with family or friends over video calls can uplift one's mood instantly.

- **Don't Skip Your Workout**

  With gyms, parks, and beaches closed, it has been difficult to maintain an exercise regime. It took me some time, but when I put my mind to it, some of my furniture turned into makeshift gym equipment. Small steps taken each day towards a healthier you can be very rewarding. But it's also okay to let go occasionally. We have been given this opportunity to make adjustments to our schedules and try out things we did not have time for earlier. I cannot stress enough on the importance of movement—be it a walk or light exercise—and eating healthy. Involve people around you to help motivate you or join in on the routine.

- **Practise Meditation**

  This pandemic gave me an opportunity to

start meditating. For me, it's about slowing down and concentrating on my breathing and thoughts. Taking a few minutes out each day to just be with yourself and your thoughts is crucial. It helps alleviate stress and brings order to thoughts that run amok.

- **Do What You Love**

  Simple things like painting, picking up a new skill, reading a book, or just listening to music can take your mind off the fear of the unknown. Doing what you enjoy can make you feel happy and relaxed.

- **Reconnect with People**

  I came across a picture of my 10th grade classmates during the lockdown. It got me thinking about each of them and how life was treating them. In all these years, being so busy with work, I did not have the time to pause and think about my childhood and my childhood friends in Shimla. The lockdown gave me the time to pause. Reliving some of life's fine moments and talking to old, lost friends, I realised how good it made me feel.

- **Maintain a Gratitude Journal**

  There is a lot to be thankful for. We take so many things for granted that we forget the impact of even the smallest of things that add meaning to our lives. Make sure you make a list of those things so that you can go back to them every now and then.

I used this time to appreciate the gifts Mother Nature has to offer—birds chirping each morning and the sky painting different hues of red and orange each evening. Where was the time to stand and stare at all this beauty before? Maybe, this was a blessing in disguise to make us realise the power and importance of nature and acknowledge what we have done to it and what measures we can take to restore it.

Spending more time with my mother, listening to all her stories, reminiscing, and sharing laughs brought me immense joy and peace. Making time for our loved ones and teaching and learning with them also holds great value. A lot of people I had talked to shared their stories of how they had discovered their partners, parents, and children all over again.

The most important thing to remember is to support each other in whatever way we can. Yes, some days will be good and some will not. Write the bad days off as a 'time out' and allow yourself to recuperate. Make 'this, too, shall pass' your little mantra for everything. But in the meantime, ask yourself, 'What am I learning from this situation? How has it transformed me? How has it reshaped my sense of purpose? What has it taught me about life?'

Lastly, sometimes we get so caught up in our duties and responsibilities, we forget that we don't have to be busy *all* the time. We don't always need to rush to the next thing on our to-do list. We need to remind ourselves that it is absolutely all right to slow down every once in a while, take in a deep breath, and enjoy what life has to offer. It's true that we all are fighting our own demons, but we don't have to do it all alone.

9

The 'New Normal' through My Lens

Weeks turned into months, but the news that 'it is finally over' never came. Unfortunately, the only constant was the rising numbers of Covid positive people across the country. And the world. Needless to say, the question in our heads was: What is life going to be like after the lockdown? With each passing week we adjusted to this new normal and it turned out to be extremely different from how we knew life pre-Covid. But after months of what people are calling to be the 'new normal', we created our very own sense of it. Many even secretly enjoyed some of the positive aspects of the situation, like taking up new hobbies, working from home, and saving the time and money spent on the commute. But this brought along the question of how will we ever readjust and what will the new normal look and feel like?

Before the pandemic hit and the world came to a standstill, most of us were accustomed to the roller-coaster life. We tried to tackle everything that our work demanded from us and kept up with all the responsibilities and commitments. Work deadlines, social and family obligations, keeping up with the newest fashion trends technology, we were always up-to-date. But the pandemic brought along a series of change with it. People around the globe took up a slower pace at life. With offices, parks, gyms, schools, and restaurants closed, we were forced to spend time indoors.

A lot of us took this in our stride and slowly, but surely, embarked on a journey of finding meaningful ways to deal with it. We got in touch with ourselves, cooked new dishes, started gardening, made time to read, picked up a new hobby, or upgraded our skills. Many of us spent time with our families by engaging in board games, solving puzzles, or setting a routine involving household chores assigned to each family member. All this made us understand and value human connections, empathy, tolerance, and resilience at a whole new level. It presented us with a unique opportunity to reflect, slow down, and consider some very valuable lessons.

During the unlock phase, things slowly began to move forward. It made us wonder if we would be able to continue these new-found hobbies and find a balance between our new and old way of life? It took me by surprise that humans have the ability to readjust, refocus, and adapt quickly. So, why not look at the positive outcomes of this pandemic and continue to work with them.

Here are a few of my positive takeaways that I feel all of us should be thankful for:

- **Time with Family and 'Me Time'**

  On the top of my list is the time we were gifted to spend with our loved ones and reconnect with them. There is so much joy in simply spending time with family members, planning various meals for the day together, listening to the treasure trove of stories our elders have to share, and watching shows or movies together. Similarly, taking out time for ourselves and indulging in things that relax and rejuvenate us turned out to be precious. Why must this stop once everything is back to normal? I have always maintained that it is not the quantity of time spent but the quality of time given. Setting aside time each week for the ones who matter the most—which includes yourself—should be a top priority. It not only gives others the pleasure of having you around but also leaves you feeling revitalised, with a sense of complete well-being, minus the guilt of missing out.

- **Physical and Mental Well-Being**

  I completely agree that since the spread of Covid-19, uncertainty has taken a toll on us. But we still fought it, and are still fighting it, isn't it? We put on the best face possible each morning and found innovative ways of taking care of our health—both physical and mental. Right from freshly cooked homemade meals—with an extra ingredient of love and care—to turning to online yoga, meditation classes, dancing to our favourite music, and making time for a walk or jog, the benefits are immense. If working out is something you began during the lockdown, make sure that you don't stop now and keep up with this habit.

- **The Coming Together of Humankind**

  If there is one thing that has helped us all overcome and fight this pandemic, it is the coming together of the human race. People from all over the globe have united, realising our strength in this unity. We learnt to let go of our prejudice, forget our differences, work together to bring back peace, and live in harmony. The virus didn't differentiate between the gender, race, ethnicity, and religion, did it? It has been a lesson to learn from: What affects and weakens one will affect all of us. This period showed us the unsurmountable efforts of all countries coming together in support of one another. The heart-warming gestures of humanity towards their own kind, and other species included, once again reaffirmed our faith in the human race.

- **Nature Is the Best Medicine**

  One thing that stood constant during our difficult times was Mother Nature. Nature is immortal and has no substitute. We get so caught up in our everyday life that often the most free and available antidote to stress and anxiety is overlooked. It is rightly called 'Mother Nature', for in its sweet embrace through the chirping of the birds, moonlight, sunset, twinkling skies, clear streams, and

> fresh air all our worries seem to dissipate. The lockdown gave me a chance to stop and stare and imbibe what our beautiful planet has to offer. While we were confined to our homes, Mother Nature healed. Let this connection that we made with her not fade away in years to come.

The lockdown offered us a once-in-a-lifetime opportunity to reinvent ourselves, unlearn certain things, and learn some new ones. It changed our perspective and taught us the value of human connection and the importance of nature. It also offered us a space to grow, rewire, and take a journey inwards.

At the end of the day, I hope that we have all come out of this lockdown with a new-found persona, determined to rebuild our identity and make necessary changes to lead a more successful, peaceful, and fulfilling life. Let us all be examples to the coming generations of what we made of ourselves, and each other, when an unknown, unseen, and vicious enemy barged into our lives unannounced and destroyed life as we knew it. I truly wish and pray that these unprecedented circumstances were a learning curve and the beginning of redefining not only ourselves but humanity as well.

Part II
Adapting to Change

10
Change Is the Law of Life

You must have come across the saying, 'Change is the only constant in life,' many a time. But its meaning holds especially true when we are hit with what seems to be the unknown. The best example of change is the pandemic. Usually, change takes place slowly, but a lot was turned upside down almost overnight when the virus spread rapidly, catching us unawares. Truth is stranger than fiction. Real stories are more exciting than imagined narratives. Before I started working on this book, I had come across a true story that resonated with me. The story is about the Choluteca Bridge in Honduras.

In Honduras, Central America, the government built a new bridge over the Choluteca River to connect it to a new bypass. Now, this is a country that is frequently visited by hurricanes, and they needed a robust bridge that could withstand all the forceful weather conditions. So, with the help of a Japanese firm, along with its latest technology, they built a strong bridge. The construction began in 1996 and ended in 1998. A few months later, Hurricane Mitch hit Honduras and, just in four days, they received the amount of rains they usually received in six months.

River Choluteca flooded the country. The devastation was enormous, several people lost their lives, and the destruction to property was immense. The hurricane destroyed all bridges except the newly constructed Choluteca Bridge. It remained intact, almost in a near-perfect condition. However, there was a slight problem. Due to the heavy flooding, the river formed a new channel and changed its course! The river that used to flow under the bridge found a new route *beside* the gigantic hunk of metal and cement. Thus, the bridge was rendered useless. It came to be known as 'The Bridge to Nowhere'.

I had never heard of or even imagined that a river could change its direction *after* they had built a bridge on it! This story stood as a metaphor of many learnings for me. The sudden change in the river's course, brought to light, the irony and uncertainty of life. Anything and everything can change without prior notice. And just like the river, sometimes we, too, need to change our course in order to keep up with the circumstances and match the ever-changing challenges that life throws at us.

Just like this river's course, things changed overnight for all of us with the rapid spread of Covid-19. The world was forced to make drastic adjustments and change how we looked at life, or for that matter, lived it. It was now more evident than ever that adaptability is the key to survival. Sometimes, these adjustments are made by choice; other times, they are forced upon us, pushing us to acclimatise to the circumstances. Resisting it or simply not wanting to acknowledge the need to adjust can lead to conflicts within and with those around us. Being resistant to change, sometimes, results in losing control or the choice of how you want to move ahead in life.

Certain life events or crisis cannot be circumvented. It is these kinds of challenges that compel us to move out of our comfort zone, thereby helping us learn and grow as individuals. The pandemic taught us that some things are beyond our control and it is crucial, even better, to accept it at times. When we let go of the need to be in complete and total control of things, we might give ourselves the permission to focus on the transition needed to accept things and move forward with the new reality. Because, let's be honest, one cannot control nature. So, it's for the best to accept it and see where it goes and what we can do to tackle it, rather than changing it. Yes, the fear of the unknown and uncertainty often holds us back, but at first what may seem fearful may well turn out to be for the best.

I believe that it is better to be prepared for change. That way, we will be prepared to work with it, thereby being in control of what we face in life and how we deal with it. Accepting change is the first and most crucial step. We must be ready for surprises and be willing to learn new things. Our resilience in life can only grow stronger when we embrace change and manage these challenges in a positive manner, rather than hide and ignore the opportunities that change can bring in our lives.

We cannot escape the impact change can bring. But learning to adapt when the need arises can very well be the key to not only surviving but thriving in the situation at hand. Our power of choice is what enables us to make positive changes in our lives. The more we exercise this power and the more we train our mindset to adapt to change in a positive manner, the more flexible we will become in dealing with such situations. We need to look for uplifting ways to deal with the burdens and stresses of our daily lives. This will be the very key to our stability—both on a mental as well as physical level.

Sometimes, we live with regrets or hold on to

the failures we have come across in our lives. These memories not only hold us back from trying again but also deprive us of the opportunity to live life on our own terms. Learning from the past, readjusting, re-evaluating, and adapting to the new will always take us forward with renewed gusto and instil a fresh zest for life. Resisting or even denying the need for change can lead to the feelings of inadequacy, despair, and helplessness.

We all wish to live happy, fulfilling, and successful lives. In order to achieve this, we need to actively understand how and when to adapt, what to let go of, and what lessons to learn from to make the necessary changes. As humans, we are constantly growing and evolving. Let us not fight making changes, instead we must learn to welcome and embrace these experiences that we come across in this beautiful journey of life. We all must learn to let go of any personal limitations we place on ourselves. It's not fair to do that to ourselves, is it?

In the words of former US President John F. Kennedy, 'Change is the law of life. And those who look only to the past or present are certain to miss the future.'

11

Review, Rethink, and Reset

The outbreak of the coronavirus seemed like an angry Mother Nature's way of sending us to our rooms to think about our actions. It's as if she had grounded us. Before Covid-19 turned our world upside down, we were surrounded by the things we *had* to do, things that were a *must*. Finding time even to catch our breaths and be able to hear our own thoughts was nothing less than a colossal task. In the uproar of everyday life, the meaning of life somehow slipped away without us even realising its value. Thus, with the initial unease and underlying feelings of uncertainty, came along a sense much-needed quietness that seeped into our minds. As the clamour of the city life was silenced, we listened to the unfamiliar sounds of birds chirping in the morning; we even welcomed it.

Yes, the emptiness in the otherwise busy streets was unbelievable, unnerving even. In a country with over 1.3 billion people, the crowds suddenly vanished, and one couldn't help but wonder where did they disappear? Wasn't it something to ponder upon? Who knew that our need to take a break and actually take a pause from our busy lives would come in the form of a pandemic? It took something so grave to force us to step back and re-evaluate. For the first time in so long the urge for solitude and stillness was answered in this form.

But look at the condition of self-isolation that it brought along with it, something that barred us from the one thing we thrive on—human interaction. The various social media platforms and video conferencing links definitely made the world a smaller place in its own unique way. It also helped us combat the feeling of loneliness to a certain point. But the joy of face-to-face interactions with our loved ones, friends, or acquaintances was ruthlessly snatched away. We wondered when we would see them next, hug them, and go out with them. No matter what the number of phone calls or hours spent over the internet connecting with each other, it didn't really replace the satisfaction of the human touch. Needless to say, we all longed to see our loved ones.

Can online classes and Zoom meetings really replace the joy of in-class mischief and the banter we share with colleagues over a coffee break? Though social media helped us stay in touch during this humanitarian crisis, the social distancing norms made us contemplate the strength of our ties. We would often crib about the long commute to and from work, but nothing can replace the friendships formed in the compartments of the local train, the pleasantness of stories exchanged between complete strangers in a shared Ola and Uber, or even with rickshaw drivers. Cities, towns, and villages wore a barren look. Playgrounds and roads that were filled with children's laughter, shouting vendors, and the rush of people making their way home in the evening were not there anymore . . . everything had vanished overnight.

But the need for self-isolation and maintaining a distance, even from our closest ones, was necessary to keep them and ourselves safe. Distance, unfortunately, became a requisite to maintain one's health. The very need to stay fit and keep going took us away from the one thing that was most important to live—our livelihood. The hours and the hard work put in to reach deadlines, the long commute, those extra office hours of toiling just to make our lives better, everything seemed to lose its importance. And we prioritised our basic need to survive. What is the value of work if we have no life? As they say,

'*Jaan hai toh jahaan hai*' (If there's life, then there's the world).

Like everything else in this world, the lockdown, too, had a silver lining. The empty streets and lack of travel was only the one side of this pandemic. On the other side, most of us were in the comfort of our homes . . . homes that were filled with laughter. Although earlier, we might have had highly networked and connected lives, most of those connections were often superficial. But the time we spent within during the lockdown gave most of us the chance to find out which of these relations actually nourish us, which ones did we neglect, and what was truly important to us? Some ties that needed extra nurturing were then blooming because we had the time to pay attention to those, while some we let go of because we realised that it didn't add anything to our lives anymore.

Even with dual-income partners, where the struggle or guilt of no time hung over like a sword, somewhere, this lockdown gave them a chance to throw the sword away and reconnect. It presented us with an opening to seize this opportunity to do all that we had always wanted to but could never take out the time for. In our need to achieve, excel, and create, we had left behind the distinctive nature of the human race. Our greed, envy, and the want to do and have *more* slowly stripped us of the important and core human values of empathy, compassion, and care. During the difficult times, the stories of humanity were overwhelming. My heart was full of joy when I came across the stories where we forgot all our differences and got in touch with our core values and stood together as one.

Amidst the pandemic, the environment also restored to a certain degree. If you think about it, the Covid-19 outbreak might have been a way for Mother Nature to revive and take a breath again. People in the northern state of Punjab, India, were able to see, across the plains, the Himalayas for the first time in decades as the lockdown led to a decrease in the air pollution. Cities like Delhi and Mumbai, too, reported a decline in the levels of air pollution. The marine life flourished, thanks to the decrease in water pollution. All over the world, the flora and fauna came back to life, the wildlife was safe in its habitat and not in a danger of falling prey to the relentless greed of the poachers.

Perhaps during this 'break', we needed to review, rethink, and reset. We needed to question ourselves that once this Covid-19 virus was defeated and the world stepped out again, what was it that we needed to carry with us? What needed to be left behind?

It is our obligation to learn from our mistakes and make specific changes to live a more fulfilled life. After all that we have gone through in the year 2020, we shouldn't just revert to our old ways of life. Ask yourself, 'Would it be fair if I did things the way I used to?' I believe that nature gave us a once-in-a-lifetime opportunity to hit the reset button, and we shouldn't mess it up.

12
Reach Out

The pandemic introduced a whole new set of different experiences including online schooling, social media as the main—and only—source of socialising, and work from home. However, it also increased the feeling of loneliness amongst many of us. We might think and feel that just because most of us have unlimited access to technology, staying in touch should not be a problem. Yet, these ways of interacting and staying in touch are mere substitutes to somewhere satisfy our need for human connection. Alas, they don't really, in a true sense, fulfil it! How can a smartphone replace the essence of a human touch, a much-needed hug, a reassuring hand on the back, and a supportive shoulder to lean on?

Some might have felt this twinge of social isolation even before the necessity of maintaining a physical distance came into play. At the onset of the pandemic, we slowly lost control over each thing that gave some meaning to our lives. To add to that, when we naturally wanted to seek the comfort of others, or hold on to some sense of normalcy, we couldn't do that either. At least, not in person. Of course, thanks to Internet, it managed to keep us connected to an extent. But as the lockdown extended, the initial excitement of Zoom calls and video conferencing soon began to lose its charm. It was even difficult for those who were living alone as social media and video calls were their only source of human connection.

I do understand there are some people who are completely fine with the idea of socialising less and having limited interactions with others—people we know to be introverts. But even then, before we had to stay inside our houses, everyone had the liberty to choose when to step out, who to meet, and how much time to spend with others. It was in our own hands to decide what our day, week, and weekends would look like. However, the lockdown stripped us of that liberty, too. Thus, at some point, even those who were initially okay with the idea of social distancing, the frustration of not living it on our own terms caught up with them. Many struggled to make time for themselves or find a quiet spot in a house full of family members who were then all cooped up together.

All said and done, whether it is living alone or in a house bustling with people, I am sure we all had our moments of loneliness and frustration. On the other hand, many took to social media, and it looked like they were enjoying their 'quarantine time' by nominating one another in various challenges, playing online games, and having virtual parties. Schools and offices transitioned to the virtual world, and so many gyms and workout sessions were held online. And in my opinion, it made it slightly easier to maintain some sort of routine. As a creature of habit, I very well understood the plight of people.

The first few months of the pandemic were challenging for some of us to keep up with. The feeling of being alienated was palpable. In the times of distress, it is a great idea to keep yourself occupied. But sometimes, people can pressurise themselves into doing too much. We need to understand that this pandemic has been a major lesson for all of us. It has taught us that we need to let go of our need to control each and everything around us as it can leave us feeling drained, anxious, and stressed out.

Let us look at a few ways we can ensure self-care and combat feelings of loneliness. While nothing can completely replace face-to-face interactions and the healing touch of a supportive friend, I am sure we can manage to do a few of these things to help keep our mental health and feelings of lonesomeness in check:

- When connecting with loved ones, make a quick check if both of you are in the right headspace to talk or connect. Respect the need for space and understand that it has nothing to do with you. They are going through a hard time as well. The person will come back after a much-needed time out.
- Look for innovative ways to interact with others. Enrolling for online classes with a friend, or just by yourself, can be one of the many ways of meeting someone new.
- If you know someone who lives alone, for instance, senior citizens or people with disabilities, it's a good idea to call them once in a while to check if they have what they need. The concept of 'love thy neighbour' has never felt more important, has it? More often than not, just a quick hello can help lighten one's mood and alleviate the feelings of helplessness and loneliness, if only for a short while.
- As far as possible, maintain a work-life balance if you are working from home. Communicate the need for your space and quiete time with your family members.

- If the feeling of lonesomeness kicks in, get up and start moving. I mean, literally move. Play some songs and dance, take a walk around the house, clean your room, or start with a light workout.
- Last but not the least, do not pressurise yourself or others to utilise this time completely. It is important to normalise the myriad feelings we go through on a daily basis. Some days you will feel good, some days you will be solemn. It is completely okay to take a break and do nothing at all. And make sure that you do not beat yourself up for not doing anything 'productive'.

We all had different ways of dealing with the lockdown. What we shouldn't forget is that while we fought our own battles, and continue to fight them, many did so silently and all alone. Things, and life in general, can be trickier when we are by ourselves, tending to all our needs without external support. But if we reach out, we will realise that there are many helping hands, waiting to provide us the love and support we need. We might think that we are alone in this journey, but sharing, caring, and merely knowing that we have someone who can listen to us or lend a shoulder to lean on—even if it is virtually—makes all the difference.

Do not hesitate to reach out.

13
Declutter

When we sit and think about it, thousands of thoughts, feelings, and emotions surround us. None of us are spared from memories. And while some memories are the ones we cherish—which give us the courage and strength to keep going—there are a few that give us nothing but immeasurable pain. I strongly believe that all the experiences—the good, the bad, and the ugly—help us become the person we are today. We don't have to like all our life experiences but, in some way or the other, they are evolving us as individuals. As we continue our journey, life's events will continue to keep moulding us into newer versions of ourselves. How we perceive these events of the past, present, and future is important. What is it that we wish to take from our past into the present? How will it mould us in the coming times?

We all cling to people, things, and places; it's human nature. At times, it gives us a sense of comfort and sometimes pain. This is called being 'sentimental'.

It is indeed nice to be even a sentimental fool, as the phrase goes. I feel that it is much better than being impassive. However, it is also true that many of our problems arise because we tend to attach ourselves to things or people for too long, way past their expiry dates. As with consumable items, even attachments have expiry dates. A common fact I noticed was that with the extra time we had on our hands during the lockdown, many of us took up the mammoth task of deep-cleaning and decluttering our homes of the extra possessions we had collected over the years. Some of it we had outgrown, some things had worn out, and some had literally reached their expiry date.

We cleaned our houses and got rid of the things we didn't want. Why shouldn't we treat our mind the same way? After all, if our mind gets overcrowded with thoughts and feelings that are doing us no good, it might just explode and send us into a tunnel of darkness and anxiety. We hold onto myriad things simply because of the memories attached to them or because we really did not find the time to clean them up. The lockdown turned out to be a good time to also revisit our emotional baggage, too.

During difficult times, it's always best to look within, do a thorough search of what serves us well, what is holding us back, and what has reached its expiry date. Working with emotions is not as easy as one thinks it is. Just like how we have a lot of mess to deal with during our annual Diwali cleaning, there tends to be a lot of mess to begin with in our mind as well. While cleaning, we jump from one part of the house to another just because we are so overwhelmed with the chaos. There are times where we feel like leaving that mess for the day and promise to clean it up the next day. But do we really get around to cleaning it the next day? I don't think so!

In order for a clean and functional mind, we must look at our emotional baggage the same way. Certain objects, people, or even events take us back to some uncomfortable feelings and memories. And at times, this literally makes us stop and ponder upon them. One thought leads to another and we get stuck in a loop, not knowing how and when to stop. The fear of dealing with them makes us leave that mess, and as a result, we end up sweeping them under the rug, promising to deal with them some other day. Are we truly that good at hiding our thoughts and feelings and tucking them away in some inaccessible corner?

Emotional baggage can be detrimental to our overall happiness and well-being. This baggage could be anything—from small uncertainties to insecurities that find their way to us. Some stem from childhood events while others from recent life experiences. But mostly, all of them lead to some amount of mistrust, despair, and the way we perceive others. Gradually, they accumulate and, probably, without our knowing, affect us throughout our lifetime. Insecurities can eat us from the inside, often draining us and preventing us from enjoying the everyday happiness life has to offer. If left unattended, this baggage can and will hinder our happiness, relationships, and the way we view ourselves. The outcomes can be different for different people, of course.

Working with this baggage is not easy. Yes, it does require self-awareness, a strong willpower, and determination to get in touch with your thoughts. But it is not impossible, trust me. Why not take the opportunity to heal one day at a time? Work on yourself, not just for those you love and care about but also for yourself. We spend all our time in tending to the needs of our loved ones, and in turn, we forget ourselves. We forget that only if we are happy and fulfilled from within can we make others happy.

These emotional distresses can keep us tied to the past. It's not possible to go back to the past and change it, but we can live in the 'now' and make the changes needed for a better present and a brighter future. As the old saying goes, 'Don't look back, you're not going that way,' so living in the present is a wonderful way to have a clutter-free mind. Being mindful of the present is an important life skill one should master. A simple task of relishing the food we eat—paying attention to its texture, temperature, and taste—helps rewire our brain to *enjoy* the food rather than mindlessly eating it. The ability to dismiss negative thoughts and not giving them much importance are wonderful ways to begin to let go of them.

Learn to detach yourself from the unsavoury feelings and emotions of the past each day. Tell yourself that you are not what happened to you but how you choose to respond to it. Using affirmations and counting your blessings, no matter how small, is a reminder that you have got this. Get in touch with your pain if you have to. In fact, write a letter to your past self, describing what you felt at the time, and write about the steps you have taken to get over it. Acknowledge the person you are today and thank your past self for helping you be who you want to be. Lastly, one of the life's most important lessons is to learn to accept yourself the way you are. Self-love and self-acceptance are crucial to understand your journey. Accept your past, be present in the now, and know what you need to do in the future to be a happy and fulfilled version of yourself.

Healing is a process . . . it is a ladder that we must climb one step at a time. But keep in mind that unless we don't take that first step, the journey might feel impossible. Just a little reminder: Nothing is impossible; even the word impossible has 'I'm possible' in it! Your mind is your temple, treat it so.

14
Discover Your True Self

The outbreak of Covid-19 has had an undeniable impact on lives across the globe. It has been a huge challenge of leaving life as we know it and getting accustomed to a life within the four walls of our house. In this new way of life, staying inside means staying safe in order to survive the pandemic. Everything, no matter how big or small, came to a halt. The ability to catch up with friends and going out for a drink or two, going for a run or a walk, and even stepping out to attend college or go to work was suddenly taken away from us. Naturally, we couldn't help but feel restricted. For some young people, the interruption was extremely challenging as their usually active and social lives had come to a pause.

Being locked up in our apartments, isolated, left many of us feeling anxious and uncertain about the future. Humans are social beings and the inability to conform to our innate nature and being all alone can be devastating for many. I am someone who is an energetic and a restless person, always wanting to be engaged in something. And I can only ponder upon how difficult the circumstances might have been for the youth. For the young adults, each day and each passing minute is an opportunity to grab the wheels of learning and ride on the waves of success. With the explosion of various sectors and globalisation, there is nothing that the youth of today cannot achieve, especially if they put their heart and mind to it. Social networking and other platforms have given rise to innumerable opportunities waiting to be explored. In my opinion, the youth are literally spoilt for choices.

It is on these young shoulders that the future of every country lies. The young and innovative minds form the basis of transformation and transition for a nation. For many, just when they might have set their minds to something after exploring and toiling for weeks or months . . . just as they were about to set sail towards their dreams, the world took a long and undefined pause. I am sure, the restless minds and eager hearts were left with several unanswered questions. I understand that it's particularly difficult to put these doubts to rest when everyone across the globe is grappling with the same situation.

But I believe that Mother Nature gave us this

opportunity to begin our journey inwards and find our true selves. As humans, we are often unaware of what we truly are capable of. In our everyday struggle to stay afloat, up-to-date, and participate in all the competitions and struggles life throws at us, we often ignore our inner voice calling out to us. This voice seeks our attention so that we can grow into the beings we have always dreamed of and aspired to be. I agree that this pandemic has been a time of vulnerability and chaos for most of us, but it can also be turned into a golden opportunity to start on a journey of self-discovery.

In the rat race of exams, competitions, assignments, and work and social commitments, many a time, the most important person is ignored. You guessed it right! That important person is *you*. It is a good time to have a conversation with our inner selves and reflect on all the things we had set out to do but couldn't as something or the other always came in our way. Sit with yourself, and in some quiet corner of your mind, you will find answers to the many unanswered questions that you got tired of asking at some point in your life.

As adults, when we are asked to unwind and relax, most of us really don't know what to fall back on. In the hubbub of life, we forgot to cultivate or nurture a hobby that would make us happy and lessen all our anxieties not only in the present but in future as well. The time of self-isolation made us face our limitations, too, as it left us feeling vulnerable and insecure. In life, there are always good days and bad days. However, both these emotions are important for us to get an insight regarding the person we really are and the work we need to do for ourselves.

Self-isolation gave us all a unique opening to dive within ourselves; observe what scares us, motivates us, drives us, and excites us; and explore the various skills and vocations needed to reach our goals. Whenever you have this conversation with your subconscious, make a wish list and create a road map on how to achieve your goals and what you can do to be the best version of yourself. Each small step will add miles to your journey of self-discovery. Now is the time to ask yourself, 'What do I wish to be?' And beyond all this, finding yourself should be fun! We all have particular talents, hobbies, and skills waiting to be discovered, which, in turn, will make us the unique individuals we are meant to be.

I hope that the lockdown helped you become the individual you always wanted to be or, at least, guided you to the right direction. I also hope that you discovered some new life skills. Whatever you experienced during the time of self-isolation will act as lessons you can apply to anything and everything you do in life.

We were gifted this rare and unique opportunity to spend time with ourselves and understand who we are, what we aspire to be, what we dream of, and what motivates us. So, let us never lose touch with our inner selves. Let us fall in love with the process of being the best version ourselves!

15
Home: The New Workplace

The reset button was soon pushed and it was almost time for our routines to be readjusted to suit the new norms. Coronavirus—the unfriendly, unwelcomed, and mysterious guest—forced us to make drastic changes. So, along with the lockdown, came the new normal of working from home. The rushed morning alarms, getting a shut eye for five extra minutes, the manic running to catch the early train, and the sweaty and anger-filled commute to work and back came to an abrupt pause as we embraced the new changes social-distancing norms brought with them.

Parents, siblings, grandparents, and extended families were brought together under one roof. Home was not just a place to unwind, relax, or simply recharge batteries anymore; it also expanded into one's workspace, online studies, and so much more. When the schools had shut early for the summer vacation, it was as if the children had hit a pot of gold. This meant playing video games all day long and staying up late watching television or just spending time with family. For working parents, this change wore a different look. They could sleep in as they didn't have to commute to work anymore or pack their children's lunches. They even had the freedom to wear anything they wanted to—even if they were on Zoom calls.

For homemakers, initially, it was a dream come true. All the family members were under their watchful eyes. The joy of eating all meals together was boundless. They had a chance to check the progress of their school-going children and catch up with them and experience the feeling of the work their partner undertook on a daily basis. However, this, too, came with unforeseen pressures. In the absence of Swiggy and Zomato deliveries, a continuous flow of hot and cold snacks and beverages were in demand—as the coffee wending machine was left in the office. The need to create long, elaborate cuisines to fill the void of restaurants and fast-food joints was also felt.

To add to the house arrest of children who were forbidden to go to the playground and socialise with their peers, it was the parents' job to fill the void when video games and virtual meetings got boring. As if this was not the only chaos to deal with, working mothers had to juggle house chores, kids, partners, in-laws, and the ever-increasing workload. The Indian household is fairly dependent on house helps, and we are blessed with the help that takes away the burden of everyday chores. The lockdown, however, snatched the liberty of having them as an extra helping hand at a time when they were needed the most. And for some working parents, it was a challenge they had dived into without any life support.

At first, working from home was treated like a romantic Bollywood movie where everything seemed bright and fun until the interval. Working from home might have given us a perspective of slowing down as we got to spend more time with our families, but it also added to our responsibilities. All of a sudden, the houses were divided into 'no-entry zones' to accommodate the online meetings and classes. Slowly but surely, the stress of working from home started to pop its ugly head with the various downsides attached to it. To be honest, the trend of working from home, especially during the circumstances we were in, was not a walk in the park.

Some of us were working from home even before the pandemic. But as the situation started to take a turn for the worse, the safest bet was for everyone to start working remotely as that would ensure safety. At the beginning of the lockdown, there was an anxiety lurking in the air, making it difficult for most people who were new to the culture of working remotely. There were various challenges to overcome. Some lacked the basic equipment needed to work efficiently—such as laptops, desks, and chairs—and even struggled to balance the finances required to purchase them to begin working in the 'new normal'.

Soon, the internet was flooded with 'how-tos' for various jobs, and people set aside some time to stay abreast with the new demands that were proving to be exhausting and anxiety-ridden. People I know seemed to be suffering from fatigue of cabin fever. They craved for the face-to-face interactions with their colleagues, the coffee breaks, and even the long and tiring commute. The routine of working remotely was nowhere close to the one before the onset of the pandemic and the restrictions of the lockdown.

The challenges were many. One's need to get things done as far as work was concerned was often flooded with unavoidable distractions. In the midst of an important Zoom meeting, thoughts of making a quick military run to buy essentials played in the back of one's mind. Dealing with energetic toddlers or helping children finish their homework became normal during work hours. There was no clear demarcation between work time and family time. The guilt of wanting to make the most of this time with family and the overbearing workload and deadlines lead to a large number of burnouts amongst the working people.

Online schools and colleges came with their own set of advantages and disadvantages. One thing that I noticed in online education was that it was the fastest to adapt to the situation. Our youth portrayed remarkable flexibility and resilience in moving with the changing times. It's highly commendable to see how educators rose to this challenge. There was role reversal of sorts wherein students helped their teachers learn the ropes of online education. This learning process set an example for all of us. However, an increase in screen time and sitting in one place to work or study took away their time to play, move, and enjoy.

I am very proud of the fact that no matter what, education did not stop. It shows the strength we as humans have within us. At the end of the day, we all made our very own new normal—be it working remotely, making time for our families, picking up a new skill, or rediscovering ourselves. No matter what it was we set out to do or achieve, it was of utmost importance to keep ourselves happy and engaged. We needed to keep reminding ourselves that this was a new time, a different time; hence, the demands of our life before Covid-19 couldn't apply here.

16
What Truly Matters

Everyday life made us almost robotic in our approach to everything that we did. We would desperately wait for Fridays so that we could finally relax. Or we would eagerly wait for the new year so that we could mark the long weekends and plan getaways. Our busy schedules, responsibilities, and the need for achievements almost took away the simplest of joys. Relationships, social outings, and celebrations seemed to take a backseat in the rat race as well. It was as if we had become slaves of the alarm clock, and by the end of the day, even a simple joy of talking to our loved ones became something that we felt could wait another day.

We took our relationships for granted. Pre-corona, whenever our family needed us, we were unable to support them fully. With the increasing distance, we lost touch with the daily happenings in our loved one's lives. Somehow, over time, we forgot the meaning of connection and family time. I am sure we all lived with some guilt of not being able to be there for them.

Honestly, I feel that the lockdown finally gave us that time to touch base with our loved ones all over again. The four to five months of being confined in one space, forced to spend time with others, after some initial awkwardness, we began to relax and get comfortable with *our* people. That time gave us the opportunity to be a family, rekindle the strained or ignored relationships, and strengthen the bond of love and care. Today, we have the much-needed time to express ourselves, be there for each other, and work through the difficult times together. For working parents, it had always been a struggle to manage their work as well as pay attention to the needs of their growing children. With a number of classes, hectic schedules, social media, and various other forms of distractions, children created their own world and often had less time or need to connect with their roots.

Elderly parents, somehow, became a small duty of general greetings and meagre check-ins. It was not because we wanted to do this or deliberately planned so, but it's just how the growing pressures of our daily living panned out. But the pandemic gave us a chance to show them how much we truly love them and care for them. In the process, we also realised that we had taken them for granted and must give them our time, no matter how the future turns out to be. I read and watched videos of how families came together over Zoom calls, played games like scrabble, ludo, Pictionary, chess, and many others. It was heart-warming to witness how family members of all ages had come together for these game sessions. Something they didn't have the time for earlier. The moments spent together over a video call—with endless banter, family jokes, and merriment—broke all the boundaries of distance. It might have also broken the boundaries of any emotional barriers created knowingly or unknowingly.

As I have mentioned in the previous chapters, our elders are a treasure trove of exciting life stories and lessons, waiting to tell us all that they know. And if we make the time to sit with them, hear them out, and share our experiences, the life lessons we may learn from them will never compare to the courses offered in any university. It is a privilege for the chosen few to have generations living under the same roof. There is so much to share and learn from each other.

Recently, a friend shared his experience of how he witnessed a teaching session led by his 8-year-old daughter, who was explaining the use of smartphones to her 81-year-old grandfather. When I heard of this story, I was absolutely delighted to know of the childlike enthusiasm in his father for exploring the wonders of technology and a moment of pride to see a young girl take up the role of an educator so seriously. Both the grandfather and granddaughter would reverse roles as she taught him about the latest technology and he taught her how to play the sitar. I got to know that my friend's father had lost his zest for life as he had no one to share his treasures with due to the busy schedules of the rest of the family members. But during the lockdown, with ample time on everyone's hands, a new ritual was found that set in motion a cycle of music, laughter, and a renewed sense of life in their house. Imagine the pure bliss of an 8-year-old learning to play the sitar from her dear grandfather! I am sure these memories will be cherished by both of them forever.

I have heard of various challenges that people started on the internet to keep themselves and others entertained. There was the Dalgona coffee challenge, banana bread challenge, and many others that took the internet by storm. Many people also turned to trusted family members for long overdue haircuts. Even in the stressful times, it was our very own family and friends who kept us going. Families came together to divide household chores, with cooking becoming a full-fledged fun and interesting event.

Spending time with our beloved pets proved to be a great stress-buster as well. We were around them for longer periods for a change. Somehow, the pets brought the entire family together. Caring for them, walking them, or even teaching them a new trick turned out to be calming. The love and compassion they bring into our lives is something I have always admired. I also heard of the stories where people were feeding strays and even adopting them. I believe that it is a model of what empathy, compassion, and humanity should look like for the younger generation.

My reason to pen down these thoughts about the little but significant things is to remind us all that no matter what life brings to us, if we have each other, there is nothing we cannot beat. It's all about how we look at it and how we choose to deal with it. The journey can be long and difficult, but with the right company and some love, it does not seem that long and overwhelming. The time spent with our loved ones, especially during the lockdown, became an important emotional memory that made it easier for us to maintain these wonderful ties. I truly hope that these memories are something we will all look back at and reminisce with a smile on our face. I am certain that these sweet memories will remind us of our strength as a family and make us realise that they are the ones who matter the most, after all, they are with us through thick and thin.

Part III
A Peep into the Future: Different Perspectives

17

For Theatre, Zoom Is the New Room

It goes without saying that all of us have been feeling restless and helpless these days. I know I am. The itch to step out has been greater than it was before. But with a rise in the Covid positive cases, we stop and think about whether going out—even if it's just to meet a friend—is worth the risk? As I haven't been able to see my friends, I am in constant touch with them through WhatsApp messages, phone calls, and video calls.

Recently (11 September 2020), I called up my dear friend and colleague, Dierdre Friel, in New York to wish her a happy birthday. A theatre artist herself, I asked her about her theatre experiences in Covid times and if we'll ever be able to perform in front of an audience? She had a lot to say on the future of theatre, and that got me thinking about how the rest of the industries were coping with the pandemic? What changes were they witnessing in their line of work? How were they dealing with the effects of Covid-19 while ensuring their safety?

We have witnessed quite a lot of things in 2020, things that we had never imagined would ever take place. For instance, the 72nd Emmys were hosted from an empty theatre in Los Angeles on 20 September 2020. Who'd have thought that there would be no red-carpet appearances in Hollywood? Similarly, the 13th Indian Premiere League 2020 (a professional Twenty20 cricket [T20] league started by the Board of Control for Cricket in India (BCCI) in 2007, got off to a start on 19 September 2020. To be played in the United Arab Emirates (UAE), across three venues—Dubai, Abu Dhabi, and Sharjah, for the first time, the only—but drastic—change was that the stadiums were empty. Can you imagine the first half of the tournament to be played behind closed doors without any crowds because of the fear of the Covid-19?

Thus, out of curiosity, I got in touch with some of my friends from different walks of life and enquired about their lockdown experiences. From a mother's point of view and a doctor's take on the crisis to an athlete's standpoint on the silence in the stadiums, the chapters in this section are the experiences of these friends. Through these chapters we'll get to know a little more about how the rest of the world is muddling through these strange times, I hope that you'll find some positive takeaways from these stories.

Let me start with Dierdre Friel, whom, as mentioned above, I called to greet her on her birthday. I give below, in detail, what she said:

> Today is my birthday. It's been a strange sort of birthday for the last nineteen years. Prior to 2001, my birthday was always this semi-non-distinct date that came and went because school had just started, and people were busy getting their new routines established. After that, however, things were vastly different. I remember that year very clearly—as most Americans do—and the horror, melancholy, anger, and pain that were hurtling around the country. People trying to make sense of things . . . trying to figure out how they could possibly carry on with their lives now that the world was so different. For me, though, what sticks out is that I had the opportunity to be reminded I was part of a community.
>
> You see, I was in school and theatre was a central part of my life and the lives of my

friends. After the events of 9/11, my initial impulse was that, perhaps, what I loved so deeply was frivolous or meaningless in the face of these world events. A group of my peers decided to come together and create a response piece to this moment and asked if I would like to join them. Music, dancing, spoken word, movement—creating a space for people to commune, to share their emotions, to begin to heal.

This experience was equally as cathartic for the performers as it was for the audience because, you see, the theatrical agreement is that the performer is giving the observer permission to feel a cornucopia of emotions. This entire endeavour perfectly encapsulates what theatre means to me.

Now we are dealing with a new hurdle in our global community: Covid-19. We are living through a time when it has been deemed unsafe to gather in large groups for fear of spreading this deadly virus. People are sad; they are scared; many feel hopeless—and the best remedy for these kinds of feelings is to gather together. This is the magic that theatre provides—a common experience among a large group of strangers. The fantasy of transporting together to another time or place. The potential to walk away having truly examined a new point of view. The chance to expand your world; to feel connection.

You might be asking at this point: How is the theatre community handling this situation? What will theatre look like in the future? Will theatre *ever* come back?

The answer to that third question is 100 per cent absolutely yes. Theatre has been around since the dawn of time. Humans need to share stories; in fact, it's a big part of what makes us human. The human race has been through plagues, famine, war, death—and still, once the dust settles, we find ways to come back together and share the magic of theatre. It reminds us who we are.

The theatrical community has grown really creative during this time in order to keep the inklings of theatre spreading to the masses. People have used technologies like Zoom to do readings of new plays and to remotely stage previously produced plays. I participated in a reading of Stephen Adly Guirgis' *Our Lady of 121st Street* where we actually had to time 'the passing of props' from one Zoom window into the next, and it worked well. We even choreographed a slap across the Zoom universe! I recently saw a staging of the number *Show People* with the original Broadway cast of the musical *Curtains* where they had employed choreography from the show.

My theatre students at New York University are blending creative hybrids of all sorts of film/video technology with the live theatrical experience. Syncing up virtual backgrounds or agreeing remotely on similar backgrounds and props that they might have at their disposal in order to create the illusion for the observer that they are in the same space or adjusting lighting to disguise various time zones. Others are claiming the realities and creating pieces that live across remote technologies, embracing the mediums fully, and telling the stories of people where they actually exist. The beauty of this moment is that we are currently realising our capability of creating art with people all over the globe!

The resurgence of the practice of outdoor theatre has been an effective tool during the good weather months. I recently got to see an open-air type of concert in Massachusetts with very particular guidelines—the audience wore masks the entire time, their temperatures were taken upon entering, performers were tested three times a week, the band was behind Plexiglas, the audience was distanced (six feet apart), and the first row of audience was twenty-five feet from the stage. It was unfamiliar, but there was a glimmer of a hope of the beginnings of coming together.

Perhaps we will conceptualise new forms of ancient theatre! The Greeks used masks to differentiate between personalities, ages, status, or occupations. The Japanese Noh theatre uses the combination of masks and strong body language to portray different emotions. In the Middle Ages, masks were used to depict fantastical or otherworldly creatures. Indonesians use the art of incredibly intricate shadow puppetry and can play with depth and space by bringing the figures closer and further from the light.

There was a very popular immersive theatrical experience in New York City called *Sleep No More* where the audience wore masks and roamed freely through a six-story building. Actors and dancers also moved through the building, telling parts of the story of *Macbeth*. All of the onlookers wore masks, which they were not allowed to take off while they were 'in the theatrical experience'. Before the shutdown, it had been running for eight years.

If I had to venture my best guess, I think we will continue to see this blend of modern devices within the theatrical medium—more of an immersive theatre experience with less of a separation between the performer and the spectator. Perhaps Broadway shows will work like a 'Pay-Per-View' where some audience can attend, and some can pay to stream live from home. Maybe, even filmed live with a multi-cam set up, so you're rehearsing it both for the stage and the screen simultaneously.

When I think of America in the 1920s—emerging from the previous epidemic—the arts were spilling over with life and colour and joy. Jazz began to emerge into popular culture (a reimagining of old classics), Vaudeville spread across the country with fervour (people were hungry to laugh and forget their recent troubles), musical revues became popular, and the American musical comedy was born. I think we may find ways to explore our commonalities as a human race and celebrate a new appreciation for the simple joys of being together.

I don't think we will move fully into this concept of people staying isolated and remote from one another. I believe that we need community to survive and to remind us of our human connection. We need to laugh together, cry together, come in contact, and share ideas and dreams. This is literally the essence of what makes us the human race. I read a study once that determined that the heartbeats of audience members during a live play would sync up. A group of complete strangers, sitting in the dark, sharing a heartbeat. Literally many hearts beating as one. What a miraculous thought!

18
Wedding Planning in the New Normal

My friend Vidya Gajapathi Raju, the charming princess of Vijayanagaram, who runs a highly successful wedding planning company, Sumyog, explained to me:

> In March 2020, life as we knew it came to a complete standstill. The Covid-19 pandemic had the entire world in its grip. There was fear, confusion, and total disbelief. Could this really be happening to *our* world? Who did this? What was it?
>
> We are wedding planners based in Chennai in South India, and for the last sixteen years, our organisation, Sumyog, has worked consistently, creating beautiful weddings for brides and grooms not only across the country but overseas as well. We had never imagined, even for a moment, that

there might come a time when our work would come to a grinding halt! No weddings were being held during the lockdown.

The people who were worst affected in our industry were carpenters, painters, drapers, set makers, florists, and even the migrant workers from West Bengal. Lighting and sound engineers and their teams were out into the cold. This was an extraordinary time in our lives where there was no work at all. And what was shocking was this virus was affecting businesses throughout the world.

As I write this, months after the lifting of the lockdown, we are now beginning to see a slow opening up of the wedding business wherein we have begun to get bookings of small weddings with just about fifty to hundred guests. This is completely unprecedented, and all of us are trying our best to readjust our thinking and plan around this new challenge. But people are still getting married, and the planning has to be conducted on an entirely different scale, keeping in mind the government advisory and the movement of our people from the warehouse to the venue.

This is now the 'new normal' phase of our lives and we need to adapt to it whether we like it or not. The pandemic has not magically disappeared, but we have to now live our lives keeping this reality in mind. With the numbers still rapidly increasing in the country, the wedding industry has been adversely affected. We as planners need to make drastic changes in our planning as well as the work required to be done at various venues.

Sumyog Weddings has made some changes that ensure the safety of both the staff and the guests. Here are a few things that we have changed, which I believe can be followed throughout this industry:

- Hand sanitisers, masks, disposable napkins can be provided for all the guests.
- Arrival times for the guests can be planned out so that limited number of people enter at one time.
- A drop-off point to be planned for the gifts at the entrance so that they can be sanitised before being handed over to the families.

- Seating plans can be envisaged with greater scrutiny and broader aisles can be planned.
- Ushers to ensure that people abide by the rules and keep in check if the guests are maintaining required distance while walking towards the couple to avoid overcrowding.
- Asking clients to make sure that the number of guests are in accordance with the guidelines.
- Install LED screens to help provide clear visuals of the festivities regardless of where people are seated.
- The number of live snack stations could be decreased.
- Separate parking areas for owner-driven cars and pick-up points for valet-parked cars. Guests to be made to wait in separate areas.
- Marriage halls, hotels, and other wedding venues must come up with attractive packages to ensure that the clients stay satisfied.
- Lastly, let's replace hugs and handshakes with a simple and cordial Namaste.

Couples have begun to plan their weddings using the guidelines laid down by respective state governments. With only 50 to 100 guests being invited to the venue, many have now taken to apps like Zoom to broadcast the various ceremonies to distant family members. The Big Fat Indian Wedding has suddenly morphed into its leaner version in this new normal. No compromises are being made to what the bride wears, but the décor has certainly been simplified and refined so that it exudes elegance and simplicity.

Our brides and grooms seem to be the happiest of all as they are now getting the wedding that they had always dreamed of! They are delighted to get married just in the presence of their closest family members and friends . . . those who really matter to them. Small and intimate weddings seem be the way forward. Through all the challenges, we are standing tall and dealing with everything that we need to do and continue with our work. For us, there is a certain satisfaction in creating these special, intimate wedding events for our clients and do what the couple wants us to do to make their day special!

19
Will Sports Ever Be the Same?

Saina Nehwal, the Indian professional badminton player, and a former world no. 1 who has also won a bronze at the Olympics, was able to explain to me the future of sports:

> I was in a tournament, trying to qualify for the Olympics. Frankly, I had a tough task in front of me. I had seven tournaments lined up in the next nine weeks, and I had to do well in a minimum of three of them. But as things unfolded, with the outbreak of the pandemic and many countries beginning the process of imposing a lockdown, we were stuck in Birmingham at the All England Open Badminton Championships. It was a period of uncertainty, and we were not sure whether the following week Swiss Open would even take place. As time went by and the seriousness of the situation was assessed,

it was clear that we would have to travel back to India and then quarantine ourselves. The Badminton World Federation had not yet decided the further course of action and the status of the tournaments that were to be held in the next couple of weeks. So, we decided to go back home and play the waiting game.

On reaching Hyderabad and being in self-quarantine, there was a sense of some sort of security and familiarity. Even staying in isolation was not as bad for the simple reason I knew I had my family around. Within a day, I was informed that all the tournaments were cancelled for the next six weeks. Although a wave of disappointment hit me, it was soon taken over by calm and peace. This meant that I could actually utilise this time to concentrate on not only my health but that of my parents as well.

Thus, the journey began. With no definite end date in sight for the lockdown, I kept busy by maintaining my fitness schedule. However, the days seemed longer and there was nothing much to look forward to. So, the motivation to stay on schedule started to wane. The idea of a match or an event brings a different kind of enthusiasm and focus in me. The rush of the preparation, the travel, and the on-court experience is exhilarating. The very idea that an event or a match has a *date* pushes you further to achieve heights and be the best version of yourself. But during the lockdown, even the intense practise sessions had come to a standstill and, slowly, the zest with which I used to train started to lose its shine. But the athlete in me and the need to be fit—which has naturally become a lifestyle—kept some of it going. I found myself pushing to do all that I could from the comforts of my home, but I couldn't maintain my pre-corona schedule. There were two sides to this situation—first, actually having the time for a flexible schedule, learning about housekeeping, which I had not tried in the past, and the patience required for living in isolation. Second, being a constant conflict within myself to stay on course when it came to my fitness regimen.

While various vaccines are still in the pipeline, we are slowly getting back to life as we knew it, trying to regain some iota of normalcy. Resuming my training was a good feeling and knowing that I could get back to the court made me feel delighted. Initially, we found a centre where only a few people were allowed to train, just to ensure everyone's safety. But as the weeks progressed, a national camp and a few tournaments were announced. To be honest, I was extremely happy to get back to training but wasn't so sure about travelling and participating in the tournaments. At the moment, I am still dealing with the same feelings as I don't know how my body will react if I get infected. Or how it will affect my family members and colleagues. This virus has been so unpredictable that, in a moment, things changed drastically for all of us. Even listening to the cases of my colleagues and their family members has been shocking and scary. Somehow, the value of life and safety not only for ourselves but those around us has been heightened during this time.

Even as we prepare for and look forward to the future, the idea that the stands will have a lesser audience cheering us on is something we will have to learn. I have not seen such a situation till now during this pandemic. The cheering and the applauds play an important role in boosting an athlete's confidence. It is going to be an entirely new experience once we get back on the court. I reckon this is something we will have to experience to understand how it actually feels. But I find solace in the fact that even though the stands will be relatively empty, each of us know in our hearts that our people will be rooting for us, cheering in front of their TV screens, and will be a part of the excitement no matter what the circumstances.

This pandemic has brought about various changes and has even altered our way of life and world view. But it cannot take away the sportsmanship or passion one has for the game. It cannot take away the love and support we have from the fans and followers. In that, I find my motivation every day.

20
Lessons in Quarantine: A Mom's Viewpoint

Sonia Dandona Hirdaramani, a mother of two, explained:

> An idyllic childhood. The cliched American dream. A home in the suburbs with a white picket fence. That was my childhood. It wasn't perfect, for sure, but it certainly was how one's early years should be—filled with innocence and naivety, unspoiled by the grim realities of the adult world. School was only closed on public holidays or the odd snow day, which we actually wished for because it meant an extra day to play in the snow. Every day after school, my neighbours and I used to ride our bikes with abandon; no fears of crime, let alone terrorism or a pandemic for that matter.
>
> My children, on the other hand, had their first experience with terrorism at the tender

ages of five and seven. The horrific Easter Sunday terrorist attacks in Sri Lanka in April 2019 hit close to home, quite literally. It took place just minutes away from our home, at the hotels we frequently visited as a family. It broke my heart to admit to my children that evil does exist in the world, and there were no superheroes that could swoop in and save us like in the movies they watch. As a result of the attacks, we were put under curfew and not allowed to leave our homes. Schools were closed for weeks, which seems like nothing in this post–Covid-19 world, but it was then. When they finally reopened, students had to wear transparent backpacks, facilitating an easier check for weapons or explosives.

Shockingly, less than a year later, my husband and I found ourselves explaining another adversity to our children: A pandemic of such epic proportions that, quite frankly, I am still trying to grasp the realities of. Conversations with my children ranged from preventative hygiene to the plight of the migrant works to daily death counts. They had encountered death at a much younger age than I did, and certainly on a much higher scale, literally tracking the number of deaths in the countries where our family members were displaced around the globe.

Covid-19 has been unfathomable to all of us. Imagine their little minds trying to grasp these uncertainties and sad truths. I had read about the anxiety that children were unconsciously imbibing from the sudden changes in their little world and the stresses that perceived around them. Thankfully, one of children's greatest strengths is their resilience. Malleable mindsets are an incredible thing.

But I couldn't stop thinking about how I could help prepare my children for whatever this post–covid-19 world would bring. How could I help prepare *myself*? The answer was the same that I always relied on when the going got tough—faith.

I used this time to teach my boys more prayers, which gave me some peace when my anxious mind began to run off to the darkest of possibilities. I read them our Hindu epics and they revelled in the stories of the gods and goddesses, fascinated by how they overcame obstacles and dark times in their paths; their favourite epic being The Ramayana. Religion is one path, but there are many avenues to connect inwardly and I believe many have felt more of that yearning during this time.

My children discovered the true joy of learning—well, when I was not their e-learning teacher!—outside of school. Now no longer overscheduled, they were able to nurture their creativity and imagination, which experts say is actually better for expanding their minds, than many of these classes we usher them to in order to keep them 'busy' day in and day out. They gravitated to new interests and passions and explored them independently.

The joy on their faces was palpable as they discovered new facts about leopards or volcanoes. They fooled around with potions and invented different vaccines, none of them viable, of course. But they were thinking about how they could contribute to the world.

I realised that this passion is the secret sauce to life and what many of us adults become more and more disconnected with as we grow older. Chores, responsibilities, and social commitments take precedence over what truly gives us joy—our passions. We get stuck in the monotonous rut in the day-to-day without carving time to lose ourselves in what we love.

The coronavirus—a stark reminder of the fragility of human life—has made it clear that our lives can be cut short at any time. Parents always say they want their children's lives to better than theirs, but maybe we should aim for them to be happier. Not necessarily having more, but maximising the joy in each day. I pray for my children to be happy and to add something positive to the world, small as it may be, and they will most likely be able to do this when they do what they truly love. This is much of a lesson for them as it is for me.

During the lockdown, I had an epiphany. I realised that even when quarantine ends, I must consciously follow a more quarantine kind of a lifestyle, prioritising learning—in the true sense of the word—practising spirituality, and more family time rather than jumping right back into that daily grind; as Anupam Kher often says, 'Running nowhere fast!'

21
Lockdown Confessions of a Teenager

My teenage friend Aahaan Arsiwala couldn't have been more lucid:

> When I first heard that schools were closing down earlier than expected, I was like every other 14-year-old teenager, excited! The idea of not having to wake up to the early-morning alarm was the most welcoming thought right in the middle of a time when all of us were preparing for what would be one of the most important tests of our school life yet, the Checkpoint for IGCSE. We had been preparing for the last three years to ace this test. But in all honesty, nothing felt better than the fact that this would have to wait. The first few days of the lockdown were absolutely enjoyable. There was no rigid schedule to follow and I could stay up late and watch television or play

games with my younger brother. Meal timings changed, and with my mom and grandmother dividing various household responsibilities between them, the luxury of house help and cooks was not available anymore. Thus, the two of us were pretty much left with little or no rules to follow.

I would often watch my mother and granny talk about the new developments and how, out of the blue, the whole world had stopped to fight this virus. In the blink of an eye, the situation became worse and a pandemic was declared. For me, it felt like summer vacations had come early. The icing on the cake was when the examinations were cancelled and all of us were promoted to the next academic year. Bye, bye Checkpoint! And just like that, the time I had once spent scanning textbooks was free and I could decide what I wanted to do with it. Was this a blessing in disguise? However, I kept very quiet about my true feelings of exhilaration.

This is how it began—late nights, staying in bed way past noon, and midnight snacking. The house was soon made into a makeshift staycation . . . or so I thought! As days turned into weeks and then months, it wasn't the same anymore. The initial euphoria of no books and no routine started to catch up with me. I am an athlete and play football for a club and my school team, too. Exercising, playing, and meeting friends each day was a big part of my life. My parents had separated recently and my younger brother and I had moved to my maternal grandparents' house along with my mother. My grandfather, in many ways, was my father figure as Dad decided to just leave without a trace one fine day. It was hard, but Grandpa did his best. Unfortunately, the year we had moved (August 2018) was also the year we lost him—on the Christmas morning. It wasn't easy to cope as my mother was working full-time to make ends meet, and I felt a bit lost. But sports and my friends kept me going. After a full day at school, completing assignments after assignments, my solace was football and spending time with all my friends. Running around like wild horses with them made me feel on the top of the world.

My days were filled with these small moments. I would look forward to the weekends so that my friends and I could have a sleepover. Mom gave me the freedom to travel to my friends' house on my own, and I started to feel that things were finally turning around for me! But with the lockdown, came the lockdown of all the other activities, too. When even stepping out was denied, the seriousness of the situation started to sink in. Zoom calls, online games, and virtual birthdays did help in managing the feeling of loneliness but did not replace the actual joy of meeting my friends. So, then the house became the place for recreation, rest, mealtime, and any other thing possible. With my mother starting to work remotely, she had one room that was converted into an office space for her. *Space* started to become a constraint, and it felt like we were getting in each other's way all the time. Frustration was the order of the days to come.

Mom and Granny worked all day to get the chores done, which left them even more tired. My brother—him being six years younger—and I got into constant tiffs. After Dad had left, Mom and I hardly had the time to talk about our feelings, and I think the three of us were just going about our days, avoiding talking to each other. Slowly, as the days passed, I began to take up some of the responsibilities at home—lending a helping hand to Granny or Mom as much as I could. I got my younger brother to be a part of it, too, and we made it into a game of sorts. Helping Mom cook or Granny clean, I did not even realise how we had come together as a unit. Over homemade pizzas and freshly baked tea cakes, we began to connect. I now see her and my brother in a different light. Board games have actually now become a family ritual, and I look forward to those nights with equal excitement as my football matches. One thing is for sure: While being homebound, I know I have learnt that no matter how things turn out to be in the near future, this lockdown gave us an opportunity to heal ourselves. Somewhere, we all just kept running away, perhaps, with the fear of not wanting to show our vulnerability to each other. It's odd but this very vulnerability brought us all closer.

Finally, my online classes have started. Although I now study from the comfort of my home, I do miss my peers and the ruckus we created when we were together. And if I must confess, I miss my teachers, too. I now realise how I had taken small things for granted—be it sitting at the back bench of the classroom and snacking in the middle of a lecture or taking permission to go to the restroom just to bunk an entire lecture. And while I sit here writing this, a wave of nostalgia, reflection, and realisation has hit me.

Yes, this virus has become an unwelcomed guest who has stayed longer than desired. But the situation it created also left me feeling grateful for all that I have. Among all the teachers I have encountered so far, 2020 has been one of the strictest. But I have also learnt important life lessons during this time. I look forward to stepping out again and going back to school, but I also look forward to continuing our family game nights.

22
Out with the Old, in with the New

A grandmother of two, Esther Sheth, had her own impressions to record:

> If someone had told me about a possibility of a complete lockdown and the world coming to a crushing halt a year ago, I would have laughed in their face and thought to myself that this person had lost their sense of reality. I mean, who in today's day and time could ever think of something like that ever happening? I have been on this earth for sixty-six years now, and in all these years have we even come close to such a state of affairs? Of course, the world had witnessed major calamities and survived wars and terrorist attacks, but it did not bring the entire globe on its knees. So, when the Covid-19 pandemic hit us and things went downhill overnight, I was totally

convinced that it was a matter of just a few days and we would bounce back real fast.

I share my home with my daughter and two young grandchildren. With their busy schedules of work, school, and various other activities, we hardly find the time to relax and be together. I looked at this as a much-needed short break for them. For me, it was also a time where I could do things at a leisurely pace. Little did I realise that the next few months would bring a sea of change and that staying at home would be mandatory. As time passed, rather slowly I must add, it also brought along countless experiences and changes . . . experiences and lessons that did not occur in all these years and the changes I never thought I was capable of making.

As a young girl, and then a very young wife, with my husband being in the merchant navy, I have had the practise of being independent and managing almost everything on my own. I brought up both my girls to be independent and free from the gender biases often thrown in by society. Living by myself was not something I was alien to. I would keep busy with household chores; taking care of immediate family members; and spending time with my children, and as time passed, with my active grandchildren. I must confess, I was a bit stuck in my own way. I have moved along with time but only enough to get by. So, although I have a smartphone and a smart TV—I wonder why it's called 'smart' as it is still dependent on a human to work—I learnt only as much as was necessary. My daughter and grandchildren would often do the other things the gadgets were made for.

However, during the lockdown, my grandchildren happily took over the role of educators and strived to increase my technical know-how. I admit that I am not a good student, but I have a new-found respect for this young generation and their minds. It is not an easy task to keep up with the number of tabs and windows, knowing what to click, when to click, and how many times to click. It comes naturally to them! I remember that at their age, my greatest challenge was to dig a hole in the mud with a stick. So, now they happily scold me for pressing a wrong switch or clicking on the wrong tab, and I get back to them by not making their favourite snacks.

Another change the lockdown brought along with it was the transition of desi chefs. As all hotels, restaurants, and roadside food stalls were shut down, the young generation at home craved their daily dose of calorie-laden food and sugary treats. Well, Grandma to the rescue! My *rotis* transformed to fancy quesadillas. Oven-baked fresh pizzas and homemade *chaats* decked up the dining table. In fact, thanks to YouTube videos, Granny's cooking also included dessert jars, waffles, and Thai and Continental cuisines. I'm sure many would agree that there is no better way to express your love than a meal cooked together. The time under one roof definitely brought us all together. Having my grandchildren around is something I am thankful for.

But it wasn't easy! The first few weeks were fine, but there was this growing sense of fear that I couldn't really put my finger on. Watching the news hours at end, one devastating story after the other, sadness surrounded me. In addition to the perils of the pandemic, so many other tragedies were occurring simultaneously—floods, hurricanes, famine, forest fires, plane crashes. I often sat by myself and wondered what had we brought onto ourselves? Did we lose our touch with humanity so much that we nearly eradicated it? Today, it's about staying away from one another, maintaining a distance just to stay safe. As a senior citizen and being at a high risk of contracting the virus, I am even more homebound. And it's just not only for my safety; I need to do this for my family, too.

Imagine, at an age where it is most important to socialise and go to the park for an evening stroll, it is time to sit back and relax. Needless to say, this year brought along with it a new set of terror, chores, and changed world view. At this age, many of us have had to relearn ways of living and moving away from the real world to a more virtual one. I don't know if it will be easy going forward, but all I think is, *was it really needed? Was it not possible to have seen this coming with all the advancement in technology we have made?* At sixty-six, I am seeing the world change right in front of me. It makes one ponder that anything can happen anytime and anywhere. And the only thing you can do is to keep moving forward. Some changes will be for the good and some not so much. All you have to do is pick the ones that suit you, accept the ones you can't change, and leave the ones you don't want. This, for me, has been the greatest learning of all.

23
The Healthcare Crisis in India

Finally, I had to get the views of a doctor, too, and it was Dr Sumeet V. K. Singhania, Consultant Pulmonologist, Kokilaben Dhirubhai Ambani Hospital, Mumbai, who gave a very interesting and frank view:

> It has been more than eight months of battling Covid-19. Both doctors and scientists are still trying to understand this disease and find the right path towards the control of its rapid spread. The fear, panic, and mayhem created by this new disease is unmatched. However, we as humans are the most evolved species in this world and we will not allow this disease to threaten our entire existence. We all are fighting back. Although the social, health, and economic aspects of our lives are disrupted, the pandemic might bring a new insight into how we should be living our lives in the future and re-evaluate our priorities.

The entire medical fraternity entered this war without knowing anything about the enemy as we had never faced anything like this in over a century. However, as time went by, we learnt more and more about the disease. There are already over 25,000 medical publications looking into the various aspects of Covid-19. Although we still do not have a magic wand to make this disappear soon, we do know the do's and don'ts of this war better than before. There are a few drugs that are out in the practice, giving us some hope, and many drugs are in the pipeline. This has resulted in a definite decrease in the death rate from this deadly disease. The whole world has come together to build a vaccine and many are in their advance stages of development that include human trials.

People have learnt that it is important to maintain their health as Covid-19 has targeted people with a compromised immune system, especially those who suffer from ailments like diabetes or hypertension. People have also learnt that obesity is an independent risk factor for such diseases. The pandemic has made us realise the importance of good health, good food, nutrition, exercise, and hygiene. We can expect people to become more health conscious and make health their biggest priority in life, which does not seem to be the case for many of us.

The Covid-19 pandemic hit us hard and fast, and the mere magnitude of the number of positive patients quickly overwhelmed the healthcare services of even the developed nations. People struggled to find beds in hospitals, and it still remains one of the biggest fears in India. The government has tried hard to keep up with the demand by opening up temporary facilities. Perhaps this pandemic will be an eye-opener for the current status of our health facilities and bring to light the need for better health infrastructure. I am desperately expecting more budget for the health services in the coming year and investment in basic science and clinical research from our government.

We have lost many healthcare workers across the world fighting this battle. This loss cannot be repaired, but we are filled with pride for our profession. I hope people will realise that doctors have gone a step beyond just treating patients to actually putting their lives at risk to treat them. It isn't easy for people to understand how difficult it is for healthcare workers to work in the Covid units. Almost all of these workers live with their families, which include children, elderly parents, partners, or siblings. The medical workers saw entire families being infected, one by one. They witnessed people dying in the hospitals who were absolutely fine just a few weeks ago. This induced fear in their minds. However, I must say that the biggest worry in their minds was not about their own chance of getting infected; in fact, they were worried about the elderly in their families. Despite everything, they embraced their work and went on without complaining. The nurses and other healthcare workers besides doctors also put their life at risk equally. In my opinion, they have been the silent heroes of this war. It is time that we start respecting all medical workers and appreciate their contribution towards the recovery of patients. I hope that this pandemic will bring further respect to the medical community and violence against doctors and other healthcare workers will stop.

It was not possible to tackle this illness without support from social organisations, NGOs, and common people helping each other. The help from the NGOs and charitable organisations have been commendable. They ensured that food was distributed to all the junior doctors working in various municipal hospitals and made them feel supported. They supplied emergency equipment and personal protective gears as soon as possible, which, in turn, boosted the strength of doctors and made them feel safe.

As a doctor, I don't just see the health aspect of the patients; their entire social and personal life comes into play. The stigma of having Covid has been a test to figure out who cares for you and who doesn't. I had neighbours coming to pick up patients at the time of discharge as the patient's entire family was in quarantine. On the other hand, I have also heard about families refusing to take bodies of patients for cremation for the fear of being infected. At one point, the pandemic questioned our social behaviour and at the other, it brought us closer together in this difficult time.

Besides tackling the physical illness caused by the pandemic, as a doctor, I am also learning and experiencing the impact of this disease on our society. Undoubtedly, the psychological impact of the entire situation has been enormous, and our culture of close-knit families, neighbourhood, and unity in diversity is the only way to defeat this disease and move forward in life. My way of looking at the whole situation is from a viewpoint of a doctor. Anupam Kher—during my brief encounter with him in the middle of this pandemic—felt that the perspectives of all the sections of society should be projected to the wider community. I feel it is crucial for broadening our thought processes and understanding the real social impact of this pandemic on every individual.

Lastly, a good life is the one where there is a balance between being ambitious for what you want and being satisfied with what you have. Covid-19 has shown us that we should be satisfied so long as we are in good health as it is one of the most important prerequisites to achieve our goals.

Part IV
Conversations with Myself

24
A Look Within

Thousands of questions run through my mind. How does one maintain calm and remain positive in a situation like this, something that none of us has ever experienced? Who would have thought that despite the advanced technology and medical research, a virus like Covid-19 would actually bring the entire humanity down to its knees. It forced all of us to stop and stay put. We definitely put up a brave front and tried our best to face the given situation, but I am sure many of us continue to struggle with this incessant thinking of *what next?*

Of course, there were times when we felt this could be the beginning of the end or that life as we knew it would never be the same. But let us look at the positive side of these strange times, too. In the past, humankind witnessed several calamities, wars, and destruction. Each of them came with a lesson to be learnt, a push to change the way we did things, and a new-found value for humanity. As time passed, we got back to our everyday lives and forgot these valuable learnings. Somewhere, along the way, we put ourselves on a pedestal and began thinking of ourselves as all-knowing beings. But this self-centredness shoved us into a new darkness. And this time, everything we had built from scratch, worked on so hard, and looked forward to was brutally snatched away from us. It was a huge jolt to us all. The pandemic, the lockdown, the self-isolation, and the basic fight for the survival of the human race forced each one of us to take account of our actions, be mindful of our thoughts and needs, and review and rethink things before moving forward.

When I sit down with my thoughts, I cannot help but think about how all these fancy clothes, expensive cars, new gadgets, and plans for the future seem to have lost their importance at the moment. Right now, it is all about how we deal with situations in our day-to-day lives, accept our surroundings, make the most of what we have, find happiness within and around us, and reconnect with our loved ones. These circumstances are giving us a push to look within and question our very beliefs, actions, and thought process.

I remember growing up, I studied in a Hindi-medium school, and for us, our superheroes were

Vikram Betal, Tarzan, and Phantom. I also learnt about Spider-Man, Superman, and so many more from friends. In the comics, these superheroes would magically save the world whenever disaster would strike, and bring life back to normal. We would look up to them, perhaps, even silently wish to meet them at some point. Over a period of time, more superheroes were introduced in these comics, and, soon, they became a full-blown franchise. Today, several superheroes rule the hearts of children and adults alike. While watching them in action, it almost gives us this satisfaction that they will appear in front of us one day, bringing solutions to all the problems on this planet. Look around . . . where are these superheroes? Is Spider-Man hanging from a skyscraper, helping the neighbourhood? Is Superman carrying this deadly virus over his shoulders and flying it into space?

No! It's us, the everyday people in simple clothing and with simple means who are fighting this war. The medical practitioners, policemen, municipal officials, vegetable vendors, and other essential providers are true heroes. We might not be able to see it, but they are the ones who are wearing the cape of heroism. Thousands of regular citizens are doing the best they can to help one another. In fact, they are going a step forward. Not only are they helping fellow humans, they are also going out of their way to feed and care for thousands of helpless animals we share this planet with. At a time when each one of us is struggling and fighting our own battles, we are making sure that no one is left behind. These people are my superheroes. The stories of compassion, empathy, and support beyond one's understanding is tremendously heart-warming. Kindness is sprouting in various shades and from many known and unknown corners of the world.

There are a few cynics and negative thinkers. They like to look at everything from a point of negativity and hopelessness, trying hard to break one's spirit or sow the seeds of doubt in others. I cannot help but wonder if they actually thrive on this way of life and find joy in pulling others in a well of darkness? The only answer to them is working harder to achieve a world full of love and compassion. We need to keep walking on this path, without a care about what anyone says to us. And when they will see that we cannot be defeated, they will join us. It is up to each one of us to keep doing the right thing even when no one is watching. This is how we'll sow the seeds of compassion and our world will heal.

If I were to look at the brighter side of things, another opportunity that arose from the lockdown was the chance to be with oneself. The everyday hustle and bustle of life almost left us with no time for ourselves, the most important person in our lives. Sitting alone, taking the time to be still and look within, the art of concentration takes on a whole new meaning. To calm my busy and hyperactive mind, I turned to meditation. I started with pranayama as it has many benefits.

Pranayama, or breath control, is the main component of yoga. The goal of pranayama is to strengthen the connection between your body and mind so that you are able to sit with yourself and slow down the desire to rush everything. This is something we all must truly strive for. A sense of calmness drowns all the unwanted thoughts. The beauty of pranayama is that we do not need any fancy equipment or a designated place to do it. Our breath is always with us, and we need not seek a special place to stop and enjoy this blissful rhythm that is present within us.

We are often unaware of our true selves and underestimate our capabilities. Often, we don't realise the potential we have to make a change or be the change. I strongly think that we all must tap into this potential so that, at times like these, we can all come together from all corners of the world and fight a common enemy. This is how we will realise the immense strength within, face our demons, bring out our best, and embark on a journey of healing and new beginnings. The time I have spent with myself has made me truly realise how this pandemic has forced us to take things slow, reflect, and come together as one global community. It is the need of the hour, and it probably has been one for a very long time now.

I reckon humankind needed a reminder that, yes, we can create borders and divide nations and claim and name seas, but it is only when we see ourselves as a unit—working together towards the betterment of this planet—can we achieve and value the true meaning of humanity. For all I know, this time around, this new beginning will seep deep into our roots, bringing with it nothing but only the best our race has to offer to the planet that has nourished and nurtured us. This is a wake-up call for all of us.

25
Have You Met Bittu?

In the last chapter I talked about how I turned to meditation and learnt to be with myself during the lockdown. Being with my thoughts has not only helped me in learning how to slow down and pay attention to the finer details in life, it has also helped me connect—rather rediscover—with myself in a whole new light.

With no shoots to go to or events to attend, I had a lot of time on my hands. The business of everyday life coming to a halt guided me towards a journey inwards, which, in turn, led to many discoveries. Sitting with my thoughts, concentrating and evaluating them, something began to dawn on me. You see, each of us have two personas. One that is innate, our inner self, the innocent, the curious, and full of wonder. The other is our outer persona, the public image we create for others.

More often than not, it is our outer being that takes over our inner being and tries to silence it. The world can be demanding, leaving us with little to no time to pause and reflect upon our life. Hence, our outer personality falls out of tune with what we truly are on the inside. We get so caught up in how we present ourselves to the world and climbing the ladder of success that it gets easy to leave our inner voice in some corner of our mind.

Growing up, I hailed from an economically challenged background and did not have most of the comforts known to others at that age. Eating out was nothing less than a luxury! But I was brought up to see the lighter and brighter side of our situation. We would laugh at our circumstances and even make fun of it. If nothing, it made life a little easier and gave us hope for a better tomorrow. I learnt to laugh at myself and make others laugh as well. I believe that is one of the main reasons behind the success of my autobiographical play, *Kucch Bhi Ho Sakta Hai*. I have always seen life from a comical point of view and, somehow, that has seen me through my toughest times.

Creativity is a way of living life that enriches imagination and helps form a connection between distinct ideas. Sometimes, it is the unique gift of creativity and thinking out of the box that leads us to difficult questions being answered in the simplest of ways. Often, creativity is perceived in a manner that leads to something fruitful, but in all honesty, it is a tool that helps us grow. As an actor, the need to keep challenging myself led me to take up various roles and push my limits as an entertainer. Each challenge accepted and completed has only increased my thirst for *more*. I have spent the last two years working on the NBC series *New Amsterdam* as Dr Vijay Kapoor. This has been a challenge in itself. As I mentioned earlier, my natural thinking is in Hindi, and here the language changes; hence, my thoughts, too, need to change. But, like everyone else, as I was at home during the lockdown, with no challenges to overcome and all the time in the world, I decided to challenge myself through Bittu!

Now, you must be wondering who Bittu is? 'Bittu' is a pet name given to me as a child by my mother. Like how in the West Robert becomes 'Bob' and Anthony becomes 'Tony', here in India, we, too, are blessed with a name that connects us with our loved ones in a unique way. Thus, Bittu represents my growing years, my childhood, and the love I have received from my family. Even today, both my mother and brother call me Bittu, and even now it contains the same warmth, memories, and love it did decades ago.

This was a challenge the actor in me gave myself. I decided to portray two different characters—Bittu and Anupam. Here, Bittu is the inner voice, which is still rooted, innocent, curious, and full of life. On the other hand, Anupam is an accomplished actor who has seen the world and is polished and famous. I wanted Bittu to be the one making fun of Anupam and his quirky ways. Here, Bittu is a guy who can constantly make mistakes, has a childlike wonder for life, and will be a lifelong learner. Bittu represents the wholesomeness in me as he has learnt the importance of honesty. He is the one who always takes his parents' advice seriously and pays attention to his grandparents' teachings with joy and enthusiasm. Anupam has learnt a lot from life as he has walked on several paths and undertaken countless journeys. Here, Anupam is up-to-date with the world and its teachings and can be manipulative if needed—as it is a skill required in his line of work to climb the ladder of success. Anupam has learnt new ways of life, staying abreast with technology and the ever-changing trends, while Bittu still struggles with matching his pants with his shoes and learning the ways of society. However, Bittu always has an edge over Anupam. Anupam may be wiser, more successful even, but

Bittu is the pure one. Anupam will always turn to Bittu in order to help him keep in touch with his authentic self.

It has been my life's motto to be the ultimate entertainer, striving to deliver the most memorable performances. During the lockdown, I started a series called 'Bittu meets Anupam' where my two sides as a person are represented. It is one of the most difficult things I have ever done, both as an actor and as a person. We usually look in the mirror to see how we look physically, but it is the Bittus in all of us who show us our true selves in the mirror of life. It is important to keep in touch with both these personalities, yet with all that goes on in our daily lives—in pursuit of achieving all our dreams and aspirations—we tend to silence our inner voice.

Trying to reach your inner self can be a challenging yet enriching process. It can be challenging simply because you create multiple identities where you wear different hats to achieve life's goals and connect with people. Each of these identities have their own set of expectations and values that may not conform to who you are on the inside. Problems usually arise when these two sides are not balanced or are in conflict with one another.

Working on this series helped me identify a few things we can do in order to create harmony within ourselves:

- Spend time recognising and reaching out to your core values—the things that take you back to your roots, make you smile, and remind you of the person you are on the inside. It can be the most basic things like friendship, honesty, helpfulness, or joy of giving or learning. Once you have identified them, take up activities and perform tasks that connect your outer self to your inner self. Start by consciously slowing down, living in the moment, and focusing on and listening to your thoughts.
- Make a list of activities that you can inculcate in your daily life that may help you be in touch with these values. Start small but start somewhere. A heart-to-heart conversation with yourself—wherein you ask yourself what truly makes you happy—and creating a road map to achieve them can honestly give you a sense of happiness and satisfaction.

- Take out time for yourself as it is crucial. A little solitude can create a world of difference. With all the roles we play in our lives, we tend to forget the most important role—the one where we are our true selves. It may sound crazy, but talking to yourself while being alone can lead to a clarity when it comes to your goals and the paths you can take to achieve them.

The world around us is constantly changing; nothing is constant. Along with all that keeps happening, we are moving constantly mentally and physically, trying to adjust and readjust to all the changes. Expectations that we build from the world and from ourselves leave us exhausted. We forget to look into ourselves. We forget that most of the answers lie within as, I believe, our strength comes from within. Yes, others are there to support us, but ultimately, it is us that have to walk on that path. Why not make time to align both our inner and outer selves? Why not dig a little deeper to find the magic within? Why not make our inner and outer selves companions in this journey of life?

For me, it was important to have a comical stance in the series mostly because when you want to send out a message to people, there is no better way than doing it through entertainment enwrapped in some humour. What I wanted to portray was that there is a both a 'Bittu' and an 'Anupam' in each one of us. While the Anupam in us pushes us to chase our dreams come what may, shed the unimportant aspects, and don new avatars, it is the Bittu within that reminds us to keep our feet on the ground. Yes, it is important to grow in life, but it is also equally crucial to never forget where your roots lie. Sometimes, we take our portrayal to the world too seriously and, in turn, remain a mere caricature of our real self. I have always fought with that feeling. The biggest joy of life, in my opinion, is to be yourself. Trust me, the feeling that comes with it is liberating. And when the world tries to bring you down, it is this joy of freedom that elevates you and gives you the strength you need to deal with it.

In many ways, Anupam may have not realised it but it is Bittu who has kept him going, pulling him out of dark corners, helping him laugh at himself, and making him believe, 'Kucch Bhi Ho Sakta Hai' (Anything Can Happen).

If there is something I would like to emphasise here, it would be: No matter how much we grow and reach the heights of success, never forget to keep the Anupam in touch with Bittu. Don't forget to stop and laugh at yourself every once in a while.

26
To Beard or Not to Beard

The sudden pause that the pandemic has created in our lives has also made us think about how we treat nature, other humans, and most importantly, ourselves. While most of us began the journey of adjusting to the situation, some also took up various tasks that involved learning some things for the first time, exploring different avenues, and discovering many things about ourselves as individuals. The initial awkwardness of understanding the demands of self-isolation, anxiety, and stress was no doubt a period of not knowing what to expect and for how long. Slowly, as the lockdown kept getting extended without an end date in sight and staying at home looked like the new normal, several things in and around us began to change. Who would have thought that in the twenty-first century, when science and technology have touched unimaginable heights, a virus would change how we perceived the world.

We readjusted our ways to fit into these new rules, rules that made us anxious or provided a sense of relief. For a majority of people, staying at home meant going natural—no make-up, no hairdos. The look and feel of natural skin has become more important than ever. We are obsessed with good looks, fair skin, and a lean figure, and living in such a society, where fair equals pretty, is harming our overall well-being.

The pressure to look good has always been there. It's only natural for us to care about it, after all. There is nothing wrong in donning our best outfits, styling our hair, and wearing make-up every now and then for occasions. In fact, spa treatments and massages are great ways to feel refreshed and pampered. But there is a difference between self-care and obsession. The pressure of always looking your best and presentable can get exhausting for an individual. And to think of it, who do we do this for? I agree, there is a sense of joy in looking your best; it gives you confidence. But when your looks and the way you present yourself 24x7 adds to your stress, it isn't doing anything for you or your mental health. The so-called flaws are, in fact, nature's way of making each one of us unique. Sadly, over time, we have built perceptions of what beauty should look like and what is ideal and what isn't—the ideal hair colour or texture, body shape and weight, way to conduct ourselves, the list is endless. When we don't fit into these 'standards', society deems us as different and outcasts us for not being like everyone else.

What we need to understand is that our mistakes, lifestyle choices, or appearances don't define us. Our nature and personality define us; it makes our identity. Accepting who we are does not mean that we have to give up on improving ourselves. If there is an aspect of our lives that we would like to change, then setting goals and working towards them is the best way to go forward. We can work for change and still accept where we are in the moment.

My reason for taking up this topic is that the lockdown, eventually, made us realise the importance of portraying our true selves and also recognise what we value greatly in our lives—and looks aren't included in this list. In fact, the lockdown gave us the time to experiment with being comfortable in our own skin. With time indoors and restrictions on socialising or going to work, many of us enjoyed the little joys that came with it—not having to wake up hours before leaving for the day, trying to apply the eyeliner perfectly, wearing the trendiest clothes, trying to figure out what to do with hair, or matching ties with the shirt you were going to wear.

This has led to people getting more and more comfortable with being themselves. That time not only turned us into chefs but into beauticians as well. This is not surprising given we have a centuries-old tradition of elaborate home remedies for skincare, but this time, we actually had the opportunity to pamper ourselves at home.

I was dappling with the idea of growing a beard as well—an idea I could not entertain all these years due to my profession. Somewhere, it feels good to let go a little. I have noticed through my social media interactions that this 'letting go' has been well accepted and even considered normal now. As people worked remotely, it was acceptable to wear anything they liked for Zoom meetings. A toddler running by or parents shouting out for meals while a meeting was in progress was something that was considered to be typical, even generating a few laughs from colleagues as this was the state of affairs of their homes, too. Another trend I noticed was not covering one's greys, thereby encouraging more and more people to spread the idea that ageing is natural, and we don't need to cover what is a natural occurring in our lives. I feel that we all are finally coming into ourselves and prioritising, all over again, all that matters to us the most.

I remember, growing up, I would see people going to buy groceries and other necessities in kaftans and pyjamas. It was a common sight. It is nice to see people these days being comfortable enough to be seen in their pyjamas to run to the local market just to pick up a loaf of bread. We discovered ourselves all over again and learnt to be comfortable not only in our surroundings but in our own skin as well.

The truth is that every human being has a perception of how they would want the world to see them. In an attempt to achieve the idea of perfection garnered from social media platforms and advertisements, we often end up feeling less worthy. It is important to understand and accept ourselves the way we are while working towards our goals and desires. Lastly, the perfect body, face, hair, or skin do not really exist. Beauty is what we make it to be. The moment we accept ourselves and be comfortable with who we are, the beauty from within starts to shine. I have always believed if you want to look for beauty, learn to see a person's soul and you'll find it.

27
Love Is the Need of the Hour

Life is not always going to be an easy ride. We all know that it is full of ups and downs. When all seems to be dark in life, everything gets blurry, hope dwindles, and life loses its meaning. Even as I pen down these lines, the grief and shock are something I am unable to deal with. On 14 June 2020, I woke up to the news of the sudden demise of Bollywood actor Sushant Singh Rajput. He had died by suicide. I couldn't even fathom the ordeal this young boy of 34 years was dealing with that made him take such a drastic step. He was such an enthusiastic, charming, and hard-working person. I had the pleasure of working with this bright and talented actor in the movie *M. S. Dhoni: The Untold Story* where I played his father. After playing a father-son duo, some of it naturally transferred to real life. Sushant was someone who was full of life, with so many dreams in his eyes. You know, at times like these, the disbelief of a person leaving sets in later, but the shock of *why* they did is louder than anything. I did not have much of an opportunity to strengthen our bond as Sushant was busy preparing for his role, internalising it. But even then, this pain of him leaving us so suddenly is intense. It is absolutely unimaginable to think about the loss his family has to deal with. There are countless unanswered questions, so many whys, what ifs, if onlys . . .*

Throughout this pandemic, I have tried to be very positive, looking at the brighter sides of things, but this news has shaken me to the very core. This period has put us all in state of loneliness. It hurts to think about how so many of us dealt with, and are still dealing with, different struggles that came our way and faced our demons. Moreover, without the support of loved ones, it became even tougher to be strong in the face of adversity.

*At the time of writing this chapter, a lot of theories surrounding the sudden demise of Sushant Singh Rajput continue to deepen. There is lot that's being said and each day a new reason comes to light. I only hope and pray that Sushant receives justice soon that—in some way—will bring a modicum of peace to his family and fans all over the world.

Now more than ever is the time to reach out and check up on your people. Nudge them to share their feelings, whatever they may be. You, as a friend or a family member, don't have to advise them, just lend your ear and hear them out. We tend to not notice the ones who are always smiling, are always strong, and those who always seem to be in control. A closer look at them might give us a different picture altogether. A person dealing with feelings of despair and hopelessness finds it extremely difficult to reach out for help; they feel that they are imposing and being a burden to others. Somehow, they enwrap themselves in a cocoon of thoughts and feelings that often take them in a downward spiral. It does not matter how successful, famous, or intelligent one is, these overwhelming feelings spare no one. After all, we all are humans—humans who need love and care. My son Sikander's words still ring in my ear, 'The need of the hour is to be a human first.'

At a time when all of us were forced to the confines of our homes, it's even more important to keep in touch, reach out, and check in. Simple acts of love, compassion, or just lending a ear goes a long way. If someone is going through a tough time, there are a few things that you can remind them of that can eventually help them deal with the feelings of desolation:

- Make sure to comfort them by telling them that they are not alone. Encourage them to share their feelings with you. They often beat themselves up for feeling the way they do and not being able to cope with it themselves.
- Remind them that you are always around, just a phone call away, and that they do not have to deal with the dark thoughts alone. Assure that you are there for them both in good times and bad. This can help them cope.
- Make them talk about their feelings. As I mentioned above, they often blame themselves or others for the struggles they are facing. Anger and frustration are some of the ways they can let their feelings out. Talking them through these emotions, allowing them to unpack those feelings, and helping them

understand a more rational way to work with them often gives them a ray of hope and some tools to work around the situation, too.

- Remind them of all the times they have fought back, gaining victory of their demons or the times they probably helped you through a difficult situation. Sometimes, they are dwelling on the past or constantly worrying about the future. Help them focus on the present as that is where the story can take a turn for the good.

If you feel that a loved one is in a constant state of misery, it's important to find a way to support them in seeking professional help. You can be there and listen to them, but a professional will be able to guide them on a path of self-healing and self-love. People who are struggling often put so much pressure on themselves to get things right so hard and fast that they may get even more upset for not meeting these unrealistic expectations. It is crucial to remind them that it is okay to let go of a few things, that they are doing the best they can and that's all that truly matters. Most people fighting this demon often refuse to see their own strength and the courage they carry within them.

Most importantly, don't forget to say, 'I am here for you. Just a call away'. We forget the strength these five words have. Say these words every day, if need be. Being there for them, without any judgment can make a world of difference. At the moment, we need to forget about earning more money, having more luxuries in life, or competing with others. What we need right now is love, empathy, and compassion from one another. We all need a hand to guide us through the dark times, a whisper at the end of a rough day saying, 'You have got this! I am with you.' Spread love and hope wherever you are. Leave no one feeling alone and helpless. After all, we only have each other.

As I reach the end of this chapter, I have Sushant and his family in my thoughts and prayers. My silent prayer is that may we never lose anyone in such a way anymore.

28
Friends—A Treasure Trove

Friendship is beautiful. Choosing the right people to be in our lives can blossom our garden of life. As Henry David Thoreau once said, 'The Language of friendship is not words but meanings'. The Covid-19 pandemic has thrown the concept of friendship into sharp focus. With the lockdown, the only social connections we could have was through our phones—be it phone calls, video calls, or social networking platforms. Yes, the friends we have been calling all these years are always there for us. But the current times have also made us reach out to those friends we had lost touch with. Thanks to Facebook and Instagram, we were able to connect with old college friends and schoolmates. And when we heard the warmth in their voices all over again, it felt like we had never lost touch in the first place and all the good times spent with them flashed in front of us.

The social connections and the bonds we build outside of our family add to our identity. As we grow up, these relationships become a part of our everyday lives—childhood friendships, friends made during college, or even work colleagues that end up claiming a spot on our friendship grid over the years. Sharing our joys, accomplishments, fears, failures, and mostly the everyday banter ensure the feelings of connection. It recharges our batteries and giving us a sense of belonging and community. Today, more than ever, the need to stay connected and hold on to any sense of earlier life has come to the forefront.

Throughout life, from grade school through retirement, our friendships become a source of both physical and mental well-being. But as life gets into the fourth gear, priorities change as we are burdened with added responsibilities and a shift in focus is seen. Like all other relationships, friendships, too, are affected—some get stronger, some dwindle, and some just fade away.

I wonder what should be the relationship between true friends? Are we supposed to be diplomatic with them or should we speak out the truth even if it means risking the bond we share with them. A generation ago that dilemma did not exist. My father's friends held themselves open for scrutiny among themselves and many sought well-meaning advice from each other. A friend was a friend forever because the bonds of friendship stretched across generations—my father's parents would know his friends' parents, and so on. Now, the equations have changed, especially for those who are successful.

The value of friendship itself has diminished and the role of a friend has undergone a sea of change. Rare is the one who seeks true friends. People who are on the top of the social and financial ladders are surrounded by yes-men in the guise of friends. The definition of friendship has also changed irrevocably as we do not have the time and energy to appreciate its value. A friend, today, in the urban jungle has largely come to mean a peer or a business associate. And as we quit jobs and move on, we leave old friends behind and grow new friendships. But are these relationships actually friendships?

I sometimes think that our times are different from those of our parents—the world is changing too rapidly and one feels like true friendships are not really needed. These are the days of 'virtual' friends and relationships. It is routine for folks to have 600, and even a thousand, friends on social networking sites. I am aghast as I wonder if all these are really *friends*? Can one be friends with a person one has never met or seen?

Why do we need true friends in these days of virtual reality? Because as you must have discovered by now—thanks to the pandemic—we all need a North Star in our lives to guide us as we sail on uncharted waters. These are the times of false values; thus, only a true friend can give us a reality check and tell us when we err. We need such friends as benchmarks and sounding boards. Even Olympic long-distance runners rely on a marker who sets the pace for them to run a winning race. When Roman generals returned from victorious campaigns, they had a slave standing next to them in their chariots as they did a victory lap around the stadium in front of the emperor and jubilant crowds. The slave's job was to mutter two words, 'Memento Mori,' in the ear of the general, which means you are mortal. It was an institution created to keep the general's pride in check.

Genuine friends understand our silence, our moods, and our pain. But most importantly, we need them to whisper the magic words, 'Memento Mori,' through life, and I think you'd agree when I say that we especially need them during these Covid times.

At the outbreak of the frightful Covid-19 crisis, while the world was being forced to retreat indoors, who would have thought that this time would also give us the opportunity to reconnect with old friends, strengthen existing ones, and perhaps even discover a few new friendships? Friends will come and go in your life. No matter how long your friendships last, the most important thing is that your friends accept you for who you are. A good friend walks the talk and shows that they care by their actions. They make the good days better and the bad ones easier to deal with. They lend us a listening ear, a push when needed, and a confidant to share life's secrets with, but mostly, they provide us that security blanket that we turn to every now and then.

Look into your treasure trove of friends—the backbones, the supporters, and the cheerleaders. Filter out those who are only there during the good times. Reach out to the ones that give you strength in times of need and vice versa. This is the time to put under the scanner the 600-odd friends' list we have on our social media handles and carefully segregate the keepers. There isn't a need to let go of the others, but we need to make it just a little way to remind ourselves who a good friend truly is.

Part V
Moving Forward

29
The War of Covid

Today, when Covid-19 is shrinking our optimism and creating hurdles regarding the basic functioning of our everyday life, municipal commissioner of Brihanmumbai Municipal Corporation (BMS), Iqbal Singh Chahal, has reinstated our faith by fighting the virus with sheer perseverance. He has made continuous efforts in making the best of everything that's available.

The rapid spread of the coronavirus came with a confusion that was enough to shake people's spirits and spread a cloud of uncertainty over our heads no matter where we went. Iqbal Singh Chahal created a major difference with his meticulous leadership skills. He dealt with every problem one at a time and was successful in developing a strategy for fighting the virus and reducing the infection rate. Fighting a situation alone isn't enough. One needs proper direction, expertise, and faith. It's a guide to survival for any situation.

A nationwide lockdown from 24 March to 14 May 2020 was imposed in order to control the spread of the virus. When the lockdown was lifted, it turned out that all the metropolitan cities were majorly affected, and Mumbai was on the top of the list. Chahal was assigned the post of the municipal commissioner in the middle of a battle . . . a battle against Covid. Changing the course of action during this battle can be akin to walking on thin ice. But his expertise came to our rescue. With control rooms flooded with calls from people all over the city and major failure of all communication lines, he changed his course of action completely and assigned officers as required to each and every role necessary.

He knew from the very beginning that they were in the middle of a war with the Covid situation. His mantra throughout was: Chase the virus, instead of the virus chasing you. His initial feelings when the Covid outbreak took place in China was that it was like a tsunami. He dreaded the virus touching the Indian soil when Italy, being the fourth best healthcare system in the world, couldn't fight it and lost many of its people. He had already created a plan in his head if the virus entered India. His foresight and years of knowledge helped him take necessary steps.

He initially closed all the control rooms and replaced them with online portals. A dashboard with the total number of beds, patients, and hospitals was created overnight. He had been monitoring the virus for 49 days before he joined as the municipal commissioner of BMC, and he had been successful in locating the loopholes in the system. His first action was to fix them and make as many necessary doctors, beds, and ICUs available to reduce the damage. With only 3,700 beds and a few ICU units, it was impossible to fight the virus, especially with the increasing number of patients.

He held a joint meeting with the CEOs of all the private hospitals in person instead of conducting it on Zoom. He took control of few of their beds and ICUs, increasing the numbers with low costs. His emotional appeals of joining forces and working unanimously towards the same goal helped him convince the private hospitals. His optimistic approach towards life helped him in fighting the situation in a similar manner with positivity and faith. In just a few days, since he took over, the doctors and hospitals were allotted to everyone who needed proper monitoring, even those who were in self-quarantine in their respective houses. Every ward officer was given instructions on updating the dashboard with the number of cases in their area and beds available.

All newly graduated doctors looking for internships were hired and trained accordingly. Later, they were assigned across all respective control rooms in each ward to monitor the number of cases, update the dashboard, check patients' reports who had tested positive and allot the beds. Every bed was numbered in each hospital, and a CCTV camera was attached to monitor the movement of doctors, nurses, and patients. The most crucial part was to control the virus in the slums. Every public toilet was sanitised six times a day, the patient's family was relocated to a hotel room for 14 days, and proper food was arranged three times a day. Only the patients with utmost need were admitted to the ICUs, and those who were asymptomatic or with less symptoms were assigned to the Covid centres built in the city.

More like a one-man army, Chahal's extensive reading of history during World War II and the Napoleon Era assured him he was on the right track of minimising the risk of the spread of the disease. His attitude, knowledge, faith in his actions, and overall positivity created an impact in the city and reduced the infection rate. There is light at the end of the tunnel, and if we look back, we are already halfway through.

30

The Times Have Changed, but Have We?

Our life experiences and interactions with others help shape our personalities and make us the person we are today. During the lockdown, each of us had our own share of experiences. Some might have seen it as a positive time, an opportunity to slow down, relax a bit, reconnect with people, spend quality time with children, develop a skill, or simply reconnect with self. For others, it might have been a forced time of solitude, or they felt trapped for weeks at end with difficult family situations or estranged partners. Whichever way the lockdown played out for each of us, it had one thing in common—it disrupted our daily lives and living arrangements in ways that none of us were prepared for.

Now that the lockdown has been lifted and people are gradually going back to work and resuming life the way it was before the pandemic, I wonder if the months-long period of quarantine has changed us in some way, not just superficially but deep within, too? As we begin to step out once again, with much caution, is our personality too altered? And if yes, how will we learn to cope with the new normal as we begin to socialise and travel once again? I am certain that the lockdown must have, somehow, left its mark on all of us. With the new set of rules for social interactions and travel, there is bound to be some change in our behaviour and how we look at people in general. After one has been inside for so long, it can feel strange to go outside. Perhaps the confidence is lost to do things that we haven't done in a long, long time.

Many would be overly concerned and anxious about contracting the infection. There is a worry of sorts that looms thick in the air of returning to the normal we had always known. In the past few months, we have been readjusting several aspects of our lives to get a grip on the ever-changing times. And now, when the time has finally presented an opportunity to step out again, we are bringing with us a lot of these new-found habits, hobbies, fears, and changes to the outside world. As we step out, armed with face masks, gloves, and hand sanitizers, the new way of interacting with people while maintaining a social distance does bring along an array of thoughts.

The warmth of a hug or a firm handshake, a pat on the back, and all such casual but important human gestures are now replaced with bumping elbows or just a warm namaste. With mask-covered faces, it has been a challenge to read one's expressions. We are now finding ourselves hungrily looking into the eyes of another to understand their unsaid words.

While most of us have put on a brave face, telling ourselves that all is fine and well, there may still be underlying feelings of anxiety, missing the way things were, and the bliss of the human touch. For people who have an extreme fear of contracting a virus or disease (nosophobia), this situation can be very challenging, often leading to more stress. Let alone people with nosophobia, I feel people in general are now constantly stressed about the complications that may arise from contracting the virus. As it becomes imperative to step out, most of us will carry this worry for a long time. The way we perceive the world around us and our very collaboration with others can take a huge turn—it is quite possible that with an ease in schedules, work from home, and virtual learning culture setting in, we might not find it as easy to get back to the real world.

Many wonder if they would now be able to keep up with the hobbies they had taken up during the lockdown or the relationships they had restored. There a lot of questions, worries, and speculations as the world prepares to step out once again. What should one expect from near and dear ones? What will travel look like now? Will we be able to maintain the positive changes made within ourselves and around us? What will the 'New Normal' look like? How far away from the old normal will it be? What is here to stay and what have we lost for good? While we all will keep searching for these answers as time passes by, many lessons learnt during these past few but crucial months will be our guiding stones to the future. Things we need to let go of, habits that need to be worked upon, and the perception of how we see the world will now be ever-evolving. Meeting each with resilience, strength, and compassion will be the need of the hour as we begin again.

31
Live Life

Out of all the conversations we will have throughout our life, probably, one of the critical ones would be about death. News of death has been around us since the beginning of this year. It makes us think what life will look like? What will we succumb to? And it's not just the practical things that need to be considered, but somewhere, the fear and thoughts of how we will be remembered by people and what kind of legacy will we leave behind? We all avoid considering our own mortality; many even think they are invincible. But it isn't so. If we have taken birth on this planet, our end will come, too. It is only natural.

I have been very uncomfortable with this topic for years and never thought that, one day, it will become a chapter in my book. Death is a natural part of life, and it's normal to think about it from time to time. But I feel many of us look at it objectively, often shunning its thoughts and telling ourselves that it isn't something we should think about or discuss at the moment. But when I hear or read about how some people left this world, after contracting the coronavirus, without even saying goodbye to their loved ones, it makes me want to talk about death.

When you are a young person of ten years, seventeen looks so far away and all grown up. As you reach the age of seventeen, twenty-five looks far. This cycle keeps going on and on. We keep looking ahead with a wish list that gets longer with each passing year, and as we tick off all the dreams and goals achieved, a new sense of wanting to do more, see more, and get more sets the pace for our life. We often tell ourselves that there is ample time, and honestly, that's how we should live life. We should live a life full of zest, not merely moving from one day to another.

Even today, when I am asked about the best performance of mine to date, my answer is always, 'I have just reached the interval of my life, let me answer that question in 30 years from now.' I am sixty-five, and by saying this, I have given myself the go-ahead to see and achieve all that life has to offer for another thirty years, at least. You see, as time passes by, it's is the body that grows old, but the mind remains young. In fact, it matures and evolves, thanks to our experiences that make us wiser.

However, during these past few days, rather

months, a lot has changed. And I say this not just about the world around us but also within us, within me. I keep saying, 'I keep running fast nowhere.' But this pandemic—which led to a lockdown—gave me the time to finally learn things about myself. With this came along some uncomfortable and some easy thoughts. And I began to look at things with a certain amount of understanding. I remember a few years ago, my wife Kirron—thinking practically—had chanced upon the topic of making our wills, but I wasn't up for it. I asked her why did we have to think about it *now*? However, during the time spent with my thoughts, I started to get acquainted with the topic. I have accepted the inevitable, but that does not mean I am left feeling morose.

As I pen these thoughts right now, I look around my room, the books signed by me, my possessions—some memories in the form of awards and pictures. I always wonder what happens when people pass away? Yes, life continues. But I still wonder what would happen if, one day, I might not wake up to see another sunrise? Who will run the school I have so passionately built? But the truth is we cannot fight death. I had read somewhere, 'The only thing permanent about life is death.' These past few months, I have lost a number of friends, great artists, and amazing human beings who will be remembered and revered for generations to come. I look at this as their legacy, the wealth they have accomplished, and the memories they have managed to etch in our hearts and minds.

As I write this, I feel lighter as I have accepted that death is a part of life. And while I know I have many more years to live, this realisation and acceptance is only going to help me appreciate life even more. I won't merely be doing things and running fast to nowhere, but welcome every experience life is going to bring my way.

Life is not just about living but all also adding life to the years we have, doing all that the heart desires, making moments count, and creating memories. I now have a new-found meaning to the words whispered by my father in my ears just minutes before he left us. He said to me, 'Live Life,' and the pandemic has helped me rediscover life's meaning in a whole new light. I now feel it might be a good time to make a will, to start appreciating the smallest of things. So that when the time comes, whenever it does, there will be less regrets and a huge satisfaction of living life on my own terms.

We all have fears and anxieties when we think about the end. Maybe, we should tell ourselves that there is much to do. Start doing things . . . start living, and with each step create your legacy. Each sunrise brings another opportunity to achieve your desires. Seize them and live them. While we cannot hide from the fact that one day it will come to an end, we can definitely make sure that when it is time, we look back with nothing but gratitude. The American poet and civil rights activist, Maya Angelou, once said, 'Life is not measured by the number of breaths we take, but by the moments that take our breath away.'

32
Living in the Present

With the onset of the pandemic leading to a worldwide shut down, it was an invitation to widespread panic, fear, and anxiety. For weeks, or even longer, depending on which part of the world we were in, almost all of us struggled with trying to get a hold of the reality—readjusting to the new normal . . . whatever that might be. In an attempt to get on with the new set of rules, while trying to hold on to some sense of the past world before, there seemed to be a huge tip in the sense of normalcy.

However, as this time unfolded, a few aspects became clear to me. First and foremost was the way in which we responded to what was happening within and around us. Stress, anxiety, and the fear of the unknown existed in all our lives, even before the arrival of the coronavirus. It's just that during this worldwide crisis, these feelings were quite evident, even staring at us. And understandably so. After all, it's not every day that life as we knew suddenly ceased to exist. The initial unsettling and the out-of-body experience started to slow down, and we came to understand the importance of *focus*. Each of us had a choice of how we chose to react to a situation and what we took away as a lesson from different experiences.

But the true way of living an experience is when one is aware, purposely present in the now, and being mindful of it. It is when we consciously live the day through all our senses, thus, becoming completely aware of its presence, do we feel what it is teaching us. And while I am totally aware of how difficult a task can be, mindfulness is probably one of the best answers to get through anything life throws at you and learn some of life's most important lessons. The definition of mindfulness by the American author and professor of medicine and the creator of the Stress Reduction Clinic and the Center for Mindfulness in Medicine, Health Care, and Society at the University of Massachusetts medical school, Jon Kabat-Zinn, is probably the most popular explanation, 'Mindfulness means paying attention in a particular way: on purpose, in the present moment and non-judgementally.'

We spend hours and days at end worrying about the future of humanity or ourselves as individuals.

And the more we give in to the hysteria, the more we tend to make bad decisions, both personally and professionally. I feel it is imperative to learn to face any crisis, especially a pandemic, calmly and mindfully. It is easier said than done, I will not deny that, but I would also like to add that it is not impossible.

Here are few ways that might help you to become more mindful of the present:

- Take a moment or two to pause during the day. Put aside whatever you are working on or thinking about and take in a few slow breaths. Notice the sensations of your breath going in and out of your nose.
- Practise S.T.O.P.: This is an acronym that stands for Stop, Take a breath, Observe your feelings, and Proceed.
- Any kind of physical movement is a great way of releasing the build-up of excess energy. Go for a walk or a run, do some stretching, yoga, or some other form of mindful movement. Play some music and move to its rhythm while being aware of the sound.
- When you are fearful and anxious, it can be hard to sleep well, or hardly sleep. Given

the importance of sleep for our mental and physical well-being, establishing good a sleeping habit is particularly important at the moment.

- Do one thing at a time. If you are trying to feel a little more peaceful inside, then it makes sense to try to control what you can control, which is doing what you're doing and finishing it.
- Give yourself the permission to feel low. It is important to acknowledge every feeling that you have. As you welcome the feelings of joy and love, you must also allow yourself to feel sad. Give yourself the time to process these thoughts and emotions. Learn from it, ask yourself, '*what is it here to tell me?*' While it is crucial to sit with your emotions, it is even more important to remind yourself not to unpack and live there. Accept these feelings, welcome them, let them tell what they are here to tell you, and then bid them farewell. Bidding goodbye to unsavoury feelings is important.

We all can step out of this pandemic more centred, in harmony not only with others but with ourselves, too. We must be aware of our surroundings, living and understanding each moment to the fullest, and taking more conscious steps towards humanity and all that it encompasses. And this way, we shall win gloriously.

33
Today Is a Gift

No matter how we choose to look at it or deal with the present scenario, one thing we cannot deny is that we are in the midst of a global trial, which has completely changed how we look at our way of life. These past few months made us face the true uncertainty that persists in life. It tested the true helplessness of the human race at the hands of nature. This pandemic has, in a way, made us confront the various aspects of life. Most importantly, it made us ask: What is the true meaning of life? What have we done so far? What really matters to us? What is it that we truly cherish and need?

It has also made us realise the value of time, how we choose to spend it, and with whom. For many of us, it might have been a painful realisation of how we have spent most of our time, running after people who do not value us much, or things that will have no meaning once we are gone. The constant planning of the future or fretting over the past often left us with little or no time to enjoy the present. We spent our time in guilt or on what ifs. For us, it was always, 'I will be happy when . . .', 'If only I had a bigger house . . .', 'I will do this after . . .'

During all this, the virus, somehow, brutally showed us how we engaged with others and that we are in an endless tug of war for status, wealth, and even amassing meaningless and superficial approvals. The time spent indoors, with oneself, made us realise how terrible it is to not recognise the value of people around us. For instance, our family, friends, colleagues, and people in general—fellow citizens and strangers who came to our aid when we least expected it.

In these trying times, I have come to realise that even the smallest gesture from a stranger, which is so genuine, has made coping with things much, much easier. As the pandemic snatched away our basic freedom of movement, it also brought to light the value of the same, something we had taken for granted. It also made us appreciate those we love, the time we spent with them, living on our terms, and the liberty to choose.

In early 2020, all of a sudden, our envisioned plans for the days, weeks, and months to come lost their meaning. Our minds raced with questions like, what were we left with? We are left with *today*. The now . . . the present. And because we hadn't conditioned ourselves to live in the now, most of us struggled with this novel idea under the circumstances. The virus gave us the gift of the present. Whether we accept it and welcome it with open arms or not cry over the plans that weren't to be is entirely up to us. No matter which way we choose to go, the fact remains that today is all we have . . . will ever have.

Think about it. What matters to you the most? Is it the past that you cannot go back to? Is it the future that you have no control over? Or is it the present? Present is where we have the opportunity to seize the moment and make whatever we do count. I find that the present is exclusive, one that we truly have in our hands. When we keep looking forward to tomorrow or the day after, joys or hardships to come, today's good and bad pass by us. As this day turns to yesterday, the regret—or the need to go back to live it once again—washes over us.

The past few months have brought several changes in all our lives. Many who criticised technology are, for the first time, experiencing its value. Many young adults and children who were lost in the virtual world began to discover the importance of the real world and real human connections. It also taught us that the world as we knew it would probably never be the same again. I am not sure whether to look at the present situation as a blessing or a curse. All I do understand from it is that, going forward, starting from today, this very moment, it is up to each one of us to be a bit more cautious, a lot more aware, and not take things for granted.

The complicated way of life loses its meaning. It's the simple things, the people we value, and the self that begins to take priority. All of us are guilty of living for the future, and while I do not wish to imply that making plans or having a wish list is now redundant, I do mean to say that through these thoughts the need to shift our focus on the present every now and then is crucial. In fact, it is something that life demands from us now. It is a known fact— and we all somewhere know it to be true— that there is no promise of a tomorrow as life can change or end in an instant. While we get rigid with how our life should be and what it will be, we often lose the chance to actually live it. Today, if we make the time to take control of the whats, hows, whys, and whens while being consciously aware to feel and take in the present, it may give us the strength, perseverance, and the much-needed satisfaction of living. Living for what truly matters and cherishing the most precious gift we have—the gift of time, the gift of today—is all we need to do now.

In the words of the enlightened Buddha, 'The secret of health for both mind and body is not to mourn for the past, worry about the future, or anticipate troubles, but to live in the present moment wisely and earnestly.'

34
The Last Day

On the morning of 10 September 2020, I woke up with a famous quote by Mahatma Gandhi stuck in my head, 'Live as if you were to die tomorrow, learn as if you were to live forever.' For me, till now, it was just a quote, but these days it holds a different meaning. I use the words 'pandemic' and 'lockdown' together because this pandemic alone could not have had this impact if not accompanied by the lockdown—a lockdown of thoughts, life, interactions, and so much more. And while they both are temporary for me, they have brought along with them some permanent impact to our lives. So, when I now think of the quote, it presents itself in a new light—it has a deeper meaning and a new perspective. Imagine if we knew that this could be our last day on this planet! There could be two ways we would choose to see it. One being looking back with remorse and regret—regret for the things we did not do, decisions we did not take, people we hurt, or simply not living the life we wanted to. The other being grateful and in celebration of life, taking the time to reminisce all that we have achieved, the love we have received and given, and the legacy we will leave behind.

Most of us live in such a manner that we have all the time in the world. We spend our days wishing for more—more money, more time, more material things, status, or power. The list is endless. In doing so, we actually put off living for another day, saying to ourselves, *I will live when this happens*. Alas! Time does not wait for anyone as the pandemic has taught us. It is when we begin to understand this reality and start taking into account of what and how we want to live, assuming each day could be our last, then we might make each day count. All the wealth in the world does not account for time. Time is truly the most precious commodity we have. How we choose to spend it entirely depends on each one of us.

If we believe that we have just one life, one chance and we will never come back and be able to have all these different experiences no matter how good or bad, I think, only then we will learn to appreciate every day a little bit more. When the pandemic first hit and we began to hear about lives being lost far away, it did worry us. But then death started to make its way closer to us and our anxiety ran through the roof. It was as if death was spreading its fangs far and wide. I remember hearing about the first case a few streets away—3rd or 5th road—from where I live, and I said to myself, *it's here, so close*.

The next thing I knew, in the building situated between mine and my dear friend Actor Anil Kapoor's house, a person had tested positive for Covid-19. According to the Mumbai corporation committee, a banner was put up stating that the building was in quarantine. The next day I heard some construction noises from the neighbourhood. When the noise got too disturbing, I checked where it was coming from. To my shock, I could see some labourers working the same building's parking lot! I was left in utter confusion and was filled with anger as to how people could have such a disregard for life. It was appalling! So, I went to an extent of telling the building secretary that while he might not be a responsible citizen, I was, and this work would have to stop immediately. He was not only putting other residents at risk but the poor daily-wage workers as well. I did this not to prove anyone to anything, but the sheer ignorance of the importance of life from one human towards others was disappointing.

In the first week of September 2020, Covid-19 hit home again. My cook, Rajendar, tested positive, and while we all went for our tests, too, the feeling of it being so close to home brought along with it a range of thoughts and emotions. After informing the officials about the new development, one afternoon, my house help, Guddu, frantically ran to me and told me that Rajendar was all set to leave. He had, in fact, packed his bags and had already left! In an example of acting out of impulse and complete concern, I ran down the street in my slippers, wanting to stop him. All the while I worried about what would happen if he reached his house and spread the infection to his family members? Then the thought of him interacting with other passengers on the train crossed my mind, and I started to panic.

Finally, after a few minutes of trying to chase him, I managed to catch him in one of the streets. I got him back home and calmed him down. You see, in some Hindu philosophies, it's the God of Death (Yamraj) who says, 'I am coming to get you.' My naïve and innocent cook happened to receive a call from the officials earlier in the day, stating that they would be here shortly to take him to a quarantine centre. Rajendar, in his simplicity, attached these words to the call of death. His panic took over and he tried to flee. He thought that this was the end for him. It took me a while to explain things to him. I assured him that they would take care of him and nurse him back to health. But I could see the fear in his eyes. He looked at me as if he was in immense pain when the officials came to take him to the centre.

I was once again reminded of how we perceived our lives when we felt that it could be the end. Thankfully, Rajendar is recovering well and all of us tested negative. These close encounters leave one thinking of the importance of life.

Epilogue

My book is almost ready. I have finally, after all these months of living the lockdown life, left for Bhopal to shoot my film, *The Last Show*. I, then, decided to go on a social media detox. It has been about ten days now, and I plan to continue it till I wrap up the shoot, which would take approximately another 10 to 12 days. Due to the hiatus from social media, a few things have come to light that I feel would be good to share. So, here I am, penning my thoughts again.

If one is to really think about it, social media is a kind of intoxication. Not necessarily the bad kind, but somewhere an addiction of sorts. Of course, it is a lifeline, too. It helps keep one stay up-to-date with the events around the world. It serves as a tool to pass the time between activities. It helps bring people from around the globe closer. At times, it overloads our mind with information. If nothing, social media has also given us a medium to share, express, and exchange thoughts, ideas, and feelings. However, along with all this, it also brings the danger of addiction and, perhaps, a false need for validation from others. We tend to incessantly check our phones after posting a message or picture just to see the kind of reactions it gets.

I remember, recently, when I realised that I was about to reach 18 million followers on my Twitter handle, I suffered from sleepless nights. I would reach for my phone at odd hours just to see the number of followers and how far it was from 18 million. Yes, it is an amazing feeling to know that I can reach out to such a huge number of people. I am sure, at some level, my posts and tweets resonate with so many. But then the responsibility of being able to keep that up, too, is exhilarating.

But in these last 10 days, I have not really felt the need to reach for my phone between shots—whether to check WhatsApp, Instagram, e-mail, or Twitter. In fact, just before taking this break from social media, my last post read, 'Temporary Closed for Spiritual Maintenance'. And it has been just that. I find myself more focused in the here and now . . . taking in the experience for what it is.

To be able to understand that one can live without a few things is quite empowering. For instance, a few years ago, I would smoke two to three cigarettes a day and would actually look forward to it after a long flight. I quit smoking about six years ago, and it really does feel rewarding to know that I can very well live without it and that, too, with a feel-good factor. It's as if you, yourself, have become a slave to a habit you have created, and when you know that you can finally quit and do without it, it's quite liberating.

I don't find myself reaching out for any device these days or think that I will miss out on too much. Sometimes, excess of information also puts us out of balance. Every now and then, a time out . . . a time to just be . . . not only helps us detox from the overload but also reinforces the thought that we are in control of what we want to give importance to. Often, we feel it is important to be present in the virtual world and participate in everything that is going on as that is where the new world is headed. It for sure is, and, as I mentioned earlier, has its undeniable benefits. But there is a thin line between participation and addiction. Unknowingly, slowly but surely, many of us become slaves of our gadgets. Instead of us controlling these devices, they begin to have a hypnotic power over us. Our moods, victories, or dejection—especially today's youths'—are all related to the number of likes, followers, and comments in this virtual world.

While it has been a journey comprising plenty of lessons, self-discovery, and introspection, writing this book has also been an exhilarating experience. To be able to share my experiences and ideas has also been eye-opening. With all that is going on around us, people have taken various approaches to this pandemic that led to a worldwide lockdown. While the underlying feelings of uncertainty and anxiety continue, most of us are now learning to accept the new normal. Covering faces with masks, carrying sanitisers, maintaining extreme caution while leaving the house, and being acutely aware of our surroundings are some of the ways this world is functioning now. In these past few months, we have experimented with various ideas, learnt to deal with the challenges, and adapted to the changing world. As we start stepping out again, following every rule set in place to a T, I am sure most of us cannot help but wonder when things will return to how they were.

I feel it is important, more for our own selves, to detox. And by detox, I don't only mean staying away from social media occasionally, but the detox of the idea that we need to be dependent on anything or anyone to add to our self-worth. Independence and self-validation are the most important self-love tools that we need to cultivate. And, yes, once we have that, it is always nice to have the hundreds or thousands or even millions supporting us, liking us, and following us. But what matters most, now more than ever, is the ability to be by yourself—living, loving, and learning life in every moment. Social media, then, becomes just another extension of our being, not our entire being.

Living life each day, treating each sunrise as a new opportunity, and being thankful for another day. Life is, in many ways, a reminder that everything can come to an end anytime, anywhere. What this pandemic has taught us is invaluable in my opinion. We don't need much. The love from our near and dear ones, the basics being taken care of, and to accept life as it is are some of the things we truly need. When one thinks of it, life is humbling; there is no space for arrogance. What are we so proud of? What is it that we will take with us? Why is it important to live in the present? Life is like a full day where sunrise is the beginning of life, bright and chirpy; noon is our adulthood, chasing our goals and desires; evening is retirement, slowing down; and then comes the night, death—where all is silent.

If we teach our young ones to learn to value each day, each moment, perhaps, the night, when it comes, will bring the peace and calm we all spend our lives running after.

Hence, in fine, I urge you all, my readers, to cherish yesterday and make today count. Let the last day, whenever it arrives, make you feel humbled and make you realise that you were the best version of yourself. Let the sunset be the most beautiful picture you paint.

Acknowledgements

This book is a celebration and a way of giving thanks to the learnings of my life. It is my journey right from my childhood—when luxury was but a distant dream—till today—when I look back to all that I have been able to accomplish. It has been an adventurous voyage of many experiences that have helped shape me into the person I am today. My positivity and zest for life began at a very early age with my grandparents, parents, and family being the torchbearers of this positive attitude. My grandfather, Pandit Amarnath, was instrumental in shaping this optimism in me since childhood through his stories from our epics. My father, Pushkar Nath, the eternal optimist, taught me a big lesson, 'Failure is an event, never a person,' and how to celebrate my failures. And of course, there are my uncles and aunts whom I have portrayed in many movies of mine as various characters; and my brother, Raju, who is one the most selfless persons I have known. My mother, Dulari, who each day while dropping me and my brother to our primary school would always remind us, 'today is the best day of your life'. The simple yet rich-in-values and shining-with-optimism childhood years is where I draw my inspiration from each day.

It is this mindset . . . a silver lining . . . even in the darkest cloud of a world of pandemic and lockdown, which helped me write this book. And here I owe a debt of gratitude to every person I have met and interacted with from all walks of life that I have learnt from and shared experiences with. I hold a firm belief that we don't meet people by accident but that each one crosses our path for a reason. I strongly believe, everyone I have met has added, somewhere, to the richness of my experiences. It is through all these encounters and lived experiences that has helped and motivated me in being the person I am today—an actor, a motivational speaker, an author, a life coach, which, in turn, has contributed in many ways to writing this book.

I am beholden for the support I have always received from my publisher and dear friend, Ashok Chopra, who is such a positive person, hands-on with life and books, and someone I have always admired; to Kirron, whom I have not met all these months but has been such a huge support, as also Sikander, our son, who has been a source of positivity and laughter; to my dearest friend Anil Kapoor, his charming wife, Sunita, and their lovely daughter Rhea for graciously setting up Friday-night dinners during the lockdown and for bringing in the much-needed love and feeling of home and family. And how can I forget Satish Kaushik, a friend and confidant, for our mundane but warm conversations during the lockdown months. I am also eternally grateful to my friend and brother Ashoke Pandit for being by my side at all times. Then there are Madan and Guddu, my domestic staff, who remained calm and helped in creating a tranquil atmosphere at home during the lockdown months. Last but not the least are the numerous friends who would regularly send me food with love during these uncertain times.

On the professional side, I would like to acknowledge Bethsheba for her contribution to the process and, sometimes, giving words to my thoughts; Mrinmayi Parulkar for helping me work with the pandemic's effects on the world; and my manager and friend, Herman D'Souza, for always being there with his support. I would like to extend thanks to Dr Jewel Gamadia for his alternate medicines and alternate medicinal treatment, which really helped me during the lockdown period. I would also like to thank all those who have contributed to this book with their stories of positivity and learnings—Saina Nehwal, Master Aahaan Arsiwala, Sonia Hirdaramani, Dr Sumeet Singhania, Vidya Gajapathi Raju, Esther Sheth, and Dierdre Friel. To Rohan Shrestha for the cover photograph and to Raghav Khattar, Sonali Pawar, and Rakesh Kumar for making the book what it is.

Most importantly, I would like to acknowledge the Corona Warriors who have been on the front line of this war against the virus, fighting head-on and selflessly, comprising the medical professionals, the BMC workers, the police department, and so many others.

As mentioned above, this book is the outcome of all my learnings, interactions, and experiences that I have been blessed to have. Each and every chapter of my life has taught me invaluable lessons. To quote Charles R. Swindoll: 'Life is 10 per cent of what happens to you and 90 per cent of how you react to it.'

I hope you enjoy reading this book as much as I did writing it!